The Cycling ANTHOLOGY

TOUR DE FRANCE SPECIAL EDITION

VOLUME TWO

Edited by
Ellis Bacon
&
Lionel Birnie

PELOTON PUBLISHING
www.pelotonpublishing.co.uk
www.cyclinganthology.com

First published in Great Britain in 2013
by Peloton Publishing

© 2013 Peloton Publishing

Typeset by Peloton Publishing
Printed and bound by SS Media

ISBN 978-0-9567814-5-1

Jacket illustration by Simon Scarsbrook

Peloton Publishing Ltd
2 Gaddesden Lane, Redbourn, St Albans, AL3 7NP
Registered company number: 7353619

www.cyclinganthology.com
www.pelotonpublishing.co.uk
info@lionelbirnie.com

THE CYCLING ANTHOLOGY

THE CYCLING ANTHOLOGY

THE NEUTRALISED ZONE

The Tour de France was conceived in 1902 by journalists seeking a way to save their flagging newspaper, *L'Auto*.

With the circulation falling, a crisis meeting was held and the paper's young cycling correspondent, Géo Lefèvre, suggested a bike race around France.

His editor, Henri Desgrange, was not initially impressed, but he soon came round to the idea and the Tour de France was born.

So, too, was the race's inextricable link with the written word. Before television and even when radio broadcasting was in its infancy, the French public connected with the race through the pages of the newspapers.

In those early days, covering the Tour must have been a near-impossible job. Daily stage reports were compiled from whatever the journalists were able to see on the road. Their stories were polished and, possibly, embellished before being delivered to an increasingly hungry public to consume with their morning coffee and croissant.

People were hooked on the episodic nature of the Tour and as the drama unfolded the press found it had the power to create heroes. All of humanity was contained in the Tour's daily dispatches.

Triumph and disaster. Hope and despair. Good and not so good.

Journalists have always shaped the race. After the Second World War, Jacques Goddet, who founded *L'Equipe,* succeeded Desgrange. He was later joined by Félix Lévitan, who wrote for *Le Parisien Libéré,* and for years the pair ran the Tour.

Very briefly, at the end of the 1980s, the race was directed by men with experience of other industries before Jean-Marie Leblanc took over and, with the bold touch of a master storyteller, gave the Tour arguably its most dramatic moment.

Leblanc, who had written for *La Voix du Nord,* took the reins in 1988 and decided the following year's race should conclude with a time trial from Versailles to the Champs-Élysées instead of Lévitan's usual showpiece on the famous Parisian boulevard.

Call it beginner's luck if you like but Leblanc's gamble paid off handsomely. Greg LeMond overturned Laurent Fignon's 50-second lead to win the Tour by eight seconds – the narrowest winning margin in the event's history.

When Leblanc retired, he passed the baton to Christian Prudhomme, who had begun his career as a radio journalist. Although his trade was not the written word, he nevertheless understands the importance of good story-telling, and it shows in the way he has influenced the design of the Tour's route in recent years.

For example, the 100th Tour features, for the first time, two ascents of Alpe d'Huez on the same day. Only someone with a keen sense of the importance of narrative could have come up with that.

This second volume of *The Cycling Anthology* is dedicated to the Tour as it marks that milestone. Between them, our writers have covered more than 200 Tours, and ridden one. In giving the writers an opportunity to tell the story they wanted to tell, we hope to have curated a collection as varied and unpredictable as the great race itself.

It is not intended to be a history of the race: rather, it is a series of essays that, hopefully, combine to enhance your understanding of the Tour.

We'd like to thank all our readers for supporting *The Cycling Anthology* and, if you enjoyed the book, please recommend it to your friends.

Ellis Bacon & Lionel Birnie

1

Samuel Abt remembers the man who ruled the Tour de France with an iron fist for years and who always harboured grand ambitions for the great race.

Felix Lévitan dreamed of taking the Tour to the United States but ended up leaving the organisation in controversial circumstances.

After more than a decade in the wilderness, Lévitan was invited to Dublin for the start of the 1998 race and marvelled at how the scale of the event exceeded even his expectations.

'LOOK HOW BIG IT'S BECOME'

BY SAMUEL ABT

Dublin, early July 1998: The Tour de France is setting up shop. Buses, bicycles, motorcycles and cars are everywhere in and near the central thoroughfare of O'Connell Street. Policemen blow whistles, officials shout orders. Around a corner trundle the three huge vans that are parked near the end of each stage to offer VIP guests a clear look at the finish line.

More whistles, more shouting, more honking. The publicity caravan begins to move along with its plastic floats of ice-cream cones and cheeses.

Sitting on a chair in the middle of this tumult, an old man swivels his head here, there, back here again, back there again.

'Look how big it's become,' he says in French. 'See how big it is now.'

The old man is Félix Lévitan, 86.

'See how big it is now,' he says again in wonder.

This is his first visit to the Tour in a dozen years.

He smiles, but does not answer, when asked if he has watched the race on television at home on

the Riviera during those dozen years. Famously dour,
Lévitan smiles a lot in Dublin. That's understandable.
He is back from exile.

The last time he was part of the Tour de France,
he was running it.

For decades he directed the race, sharing duties
with Jacques Goddet. Asked once how they divided
their responsibilities, Lévitan replied, 'It's easy. I'm
in charge.'

Not really, but close. The aristocratic Goddet had
better credentials: he was the editor of the sports
newspaper *L'Equipe*, which was owned by the same
people who owned the Tour, while Lévitan was
editor of the downmarket *Parisien Libéré*; Goddet
wrote a flinty and authoritative column in *L'Equipe*
during the race while Lévitan rarely offered a public
comment. He was the manager, the business force,
Goddet the tactician and inspirational force.

Goddet also had seniority, having directed the
Tour since 1936. Returning from a prisoner-of-war
camp, Lévitan joined the race organisation in 1947
and began to climb the ladder. In 1962 he became
Goddet's deputy, and in 1978 his equal. When Goddet
retired in 1987 at the age of 82, Lévitan, then 76, was
expected to rule alone.

Then, one winter morning that year, he arrived
at the door to his office in Paris to find the lock
changed and a French court official waiting with a
search warrant to look through filing cabinets and

desk drawers. An audit of the Tour's books indicated that, as managing agent of the Société du Tour de France, Lévitan had secretly used corporate funds to cover a big deficit for the 1983 Tour of America – a three-day race, despite the name.

Did he, didn't he? That never became clear in public, especially after the case was settled – 'to every-body's satisfaction', as *L'Equipe* put it – in 1990. The few facts that emerged showed that Lévitan had not enriched himself in a complicated television-rights deal but had tried to rescue the indebted Tour of America as part of his dream of vastly international bicycle racing. The manager was also a visionary.

While others resisted, he introduced the women's Tour de France in 1984; two years after he was gone, so was it. When Goddet called in 1982 for a return to national teams every four years, Lévitan pushed instead for the inclusion of amateur teams. He won, and the Colombians arrived in 1983 to begin domi-nating mountain stages.

Lévitan talked of a possible start in Japan or the United States, of teams entering from Eastern Europe, of stages in Moscow or Warsaw. He was fascinated by the lure of the American market, float-ing plans for a Tour of Florida in 1980 and for a Tour of California in 1981. No wonder he signed up as a consultant for the Tour of America in 1983 and then tried to balance its books.

For a man of global vision, though, he wasn't

much of a businessman. Until 1974, he revealed in
his defence when he was fired, the Tour was annu-
ally in the red. In the next decade, he said proudly,
it made a profit of $3million – just peanuts, but not
to him. He never bothered about seeking big money
for television rights; he was a newspaper man who
did not anticipate his audience's shift to television in
those distant days when few Frenchmen owned a set.
Want to know who was doing what in the race? Read
about it in *L'Equipe* or *Le Parisien*.

Nor did he try to attract big corporate sponsors.
He thought small, satisfied with the income from
the publicity caravan that preceded the race with its
swarm of hucksters for soap, sausages and sweets.
His idea of a good time for the fans when the Tour
pulled into town was a free evening performance by
a singer and an accordion player before a sheet was
rigged and, as moths danced in the beam, a camera
showed a silent newsreel of an earlier stage.

Moths danced in the beam! How could Lévitan
run the Tour de France like a mom and pop store?
For a start, overheads were low: prize money was
slight. Teams were charged for their food and hotels,
which often turned out to be forlorn places beside
noisy highways, or school dormitories emptied for
the summer. (Watch Sean Kelly wash his jersey in the
sink while others line up behind him for their turn
before the tepid water runs out.) The next morning
always began early – often at 9am, not the noon of

today's race – since Lévitan liked to cram two stages into the day, the better to charge for two starts and two finishes. In 1978, the riders went on strike, walking their bicycles across the finish line one day, to protest the packed schedule, long transfers and early starts. Lévitan backed down only slightly.

It was just as dismal for reporters. The typical press room was often an open-sided cattle market with banks of wooden tables and benches that were moved from one small town to another. That was not altogether a bad thing: sitting cheek by jowl, the 30 or 40 reporters got to know each other, which led to helping each other. At my first Tour, in 1977, the generous Emile Besson, correspondent for the French Communist newspaper *L'Humanité*, noticed that I was staring at my typewriter, unable to write anything because I didn't know anything.

I was as green as a pea.

'Say something about Didi Thurau, the German,' he prompted.

Quickly, I shuffled through some notes.

'But he's only 22 years old,' I said, 'and this is his first Tour. Shouldn't I write about Eddy Merckx instead?'

That Merckx had won five Tours was one of the few facts I knew.

'No,' Emile replied. 'Merckx is finished. Thurau will open some eyes. He won't win, no, but he will animate the race for a while.'

So I wrote about Thurau, predicting that he would animate the race for a while and proclaiming that Merckx was finished. Which is exactly how it turned out. Thurau won the prologue, took the yellow jersey for a couple of weeks and finally finished fifth overall with five stage victories.

Merckx struggled badly in what turned out to be his last Tour. Knowing that I had never covered a bicycle race before, my editor complimented me on being such a quick study. So I stayed in close touch with Emile Besson thereafter.

He may have been in the group on a stage up to Alpe d'Huez, when the French journalists I was accompanying decided to speed ahead and have lunch at a favourite roadside restaurant. By the time we had finished, the Tour, on a fast pace, had sped by. We climbed back into our car and took off, catching the pack on the climb through the 21 hairpin curves.

Horn blaring, we wove through the riders and got a first-hand view of their torment. Try that trick of riding through the pack now and the *Garde Républicaine* motorcycle policemen who swarm the route will probably shoot your tyres out.

Lévitan, in his car just ahead of the pack, had not a word to say about our tactics. As a former cycling correspondent himself – he began at age 17 – he might have been part of similar escapades.

They disappeared as the press corps grew from the 30 or 40 reporters and a few photographers to the 300 or 400 full-time now, plus hundreds of others on a daily basis from regional newspapers when the Tour enters their circulation area, not to mention the myriad bloggers. Back then it was difficult to gain accreditation as a member of the working press, wearing the green badge around the neck that allows access to the *salle de presse*.

And what press rooms they were under Lévitan! Like the team hotels, they were inconvenient, noisy and dank. The worst of them all was in Pau, where the tables and benches were installed outside what smelled like a chicken slaughterhouse and under a tin roof that magnified the blazing sun. Now the press works in Pau's air-conditioned casino, which Lévitan would have considered too big an expense.

Any expense, for that matter, was too big. The Tour's budget for 1987, he pointed out, was $2.5million or just $500,000 more than the prize list alone now. The money came from the many cities and towns eager to play host to the Tour. It was, when all was said and done, the world's greatest bicycle race. From West Berlin, Lévitan wrung the astonishing sum of $1.5million to stage the 1987 start.

'Look how big it's become,' the old man says in Dublin. He is there as a guest of Jean-Marie Leblanc, who has Lévitan's old job of Tour director and who knows him as a former rider, then cycling correspondent for *L'Equipe* and editor of *Vélo* maga-zine. Leblanc is kindly. After a dozen years of official indifference, he decided that the Tour should pay its respects to Lévitan, who is, you know, 86 years old.

By then, much of Lévitan's imprint on the Tour had been undone. His immediate successor, Jean-François Naquet-Radiguet, a former sales manager for a cognac manufacturer, said he was stunned by the race's infrastructure.

'I had a very traumatic experience,' he admitted. 'I had all the equipment we have on the arrival line put together in a parking lot – the stands, the finish line, everything. Dramatic! When you see it without the noise, the people, it's a mess. It's cheap looking.'

It all had to go. In time, there arrived huge television screens near the finish line for hoi polloi to view the action down the road plus the three VIP viewing stands, named Le Tourmalet and L'Izoard, after two of the race's majestic mountains and, more prosaically, Club Tour de France.

Then there were the television rights.

'In the income statement of the Tour de France,' Naquet-Radiguet continued, 'until very lately, TV rights did not appear. They were not important. Lévitan was talented at obtaining money from host cities and sponsors, but the economics of a modern sporting event were fairly out of his understanding.'

Although global television rights soared under his control, Naquet-Radiguet tried to go too far too fast. He was replaced after a year by a functionary, Jean-Pierre Courcol, who was swamped by the Pedro

Delgado doping scandal in 1988 and undermined his position by having *L'Equipe* print his signed appraisal of that Tour with the headline, 'I'm Ashamed'.

A few months later, Leblanc was named general manager. One of his first acts was to upgrade the prize list by abolishing many of the minor rider classifications Lévitan had introduced and by substituting money for the tacky vacation bungalows that had gone to winners. Leblanc himself retired in 2005, two years before Lévitan died at the age of 95.

Only old-timers remember Lévitan now. His main legacy to the Tour consists of two bits of showmanship so unlike his own sombre manner: in 1975 he introduced the climber's jersey, white with red dots, which he designed himself; in the same year he moved the finish in Paris from the outlying Parc des Princes to the Avenue of the Champs-Élysées, where a crowd usually estimated at half a million turns out late every July to watch the Tour.

What would Lévitan have to say about such an annual spectacle in the heart of Paris? As they were in Dublin, his words might be: 'Look how big it's become. See how big it is now.'

Samuel Abt is the first American to be awarded the Tour de France medal for service to the race. He began writing about bicycle racing in 1977 for the *International Herald Tribune* and the *New York Times* and covered the Tour 32 times. In 2012 he entered hyperspace with a Tour blog for *bicycling.com*. Now retired as a newspaperman, he lives in France.

2

Ned Boulting is a familiar face to cycling fans in Britain.

Each July, those who sit down to watch the daily despatches from the Tour on ITV welcome him, and a little bit of France, into their homes.

Meet Brian Venner, whose name may be less well-known, but who had the vision and determination to put the Tour de France on British television in the 1980s.

A LIFE OF BRIAN

BY NED BOULTING

It was almost exactly a decade ago that I first heard Brian Venner's voice. It changed my life.

I was walking down a flight of stairs, having just interviewed Gordon Strachan at Southampton Football Club a few weeks before their appearance in the 2003 FA Cup Final. The fiery Scotsman had been in a particularly belligerent mood; prickly, unhelpful and abrasive.

I hadn't enjoyed our allotted 20 minutes, and was now heading, rather gloomily, to my car for the drive home. At that point, my phone rang.

'Hello?' Or, perhaps, more accurately, 'Heeellloooooo!' How do you transcribe a single word so elongated that it seemed to last as long as most self-respecting sentences? That's how Brian talks, sometimes, when he's being expansive.

'Hello? Is that, err, Ned?' It was a distant voice, polished to within an inch of its life. It sounded as if he were shouting at the receiver through a megaphone from across the other side of the room, or as if he were calling from an Antarctic research station in the middle of a snowstorm, rather than a small office in Surrey.

'Speaking. Go ahead.' I replied, slipping comfortably into a parody of a conversation between two officers on the bridge of a submarine accompanying a North Atlantic convoy.

'Oh good. My name is Brian Venner,' said the voice, elaborately, slowly. 'I'd very much like you to join us on the Tour de France.'

I stopped my descent of the stairs mid-step. Did he just say 'the Tour de France?' I listened acutely to what he went on to say.

* * *

Ten years, and ten Tours, later, I still find myself listening to what he has to say. After all, he's Brian Venner. He's the man who, throughout the entire span of Tour coverage on British TV, has been its executive producer. It's been his gig, and, in name, it still is. You won't perhaps have heard of him, unless you are a particularly detailed student of television history. But the very fact that you are reading this book, and therefore, one can assume, have a more than passing interest in the Tour de France, may well, to some degree, be because of this man's persuasiveness, drive, particular charm, and staying power.

A recent memory of Brian. We had finished our final ITV broadcast of the 2012 Tour de France from the Champs-Élysées, and had soaked in the sights and sounds of Britain's singular win in a century of trying. Brian Venner, at nearly 80, was clothed in a white suit and panama hat, as if he were touring Tuscany with a Baedeker guidebook in one hand, rather than sharing a slightly grubby cab with me to the Gare du Nord. He looked, well, splendidly British.

We were booked on the same Eurostar back to London. Arriving to the prodigious chaos outside the shabby old station with more than an hour to spare before our train, I gently (actually, on reflection, rather forcibly) persuaded Brian that our time would be best spent drinking cold beer at one of those unappealing brasseries that face the main entrance. We started to negotiate our way across the free-for-all of taxis pulling up outside the station, disgorging passengers and pulling away again. The place was crawling with British cycling fans, partly clad in yellow jersey tat, partly sporting replica Team Sky merchandise, and often emblazoned with some artfully engineered Union Jack nonsense: a bandana, a plastic bowler hat, boxer shorts – stuff you'd normally associate with stag parties, not bike races.

We sat down at the only two seats available outside the only bar with any spare capacity, and ordered two *pressions*. A group of policemen from Kent, in their late 30s, sat next to us, glugging their way through a remarkable procession of bottles of dry white wine. They were in merry spirits, and they were instantly

friendly, all in their matching kits from some dubious
cycling club which went by the name of The Rascals
or The Ruffians or some such.

Once we had struck up a conversation (or, more
accurately, they had struck up a conversation), they
quite naturally wanted to know everything about
the television coverage. This being their first trip to
France to watch the race with their own eyes, their
only experience of the race up till now had been at
home, watching the evening highlights shows on TV.
And this year, more than most, the entire month of
July for these men had been dictated by the need to
avoid finding out about the result of each day's stage
until they could sit down at precisely seven o'clock,
to get their fix of the Tour de France. To put it
bluntly, they had watched our every move.

Now, suddenly, they had no need to sit at home
and watch my final report on Bradley Wiggins winning the time trial in Chartres. I was sitting next to
them in a bar, so they could ask me themselves.

But it wasn't long before I was able to take a back
seat in the conversation altogether. I introduced
them to Brian Venner, not only as the man who had
produced British TV coverage of the Tour de France
for as long as there had been any, but also as the man
who, in the late 1970s, had brought them *Superstars*,
Brian Jacks, squat thrusts, and all.

Their eyes went out on stalks. Never mind Bradley Wiggins. This was a revelation. *Superstars*! What

memories. What innocence. What a bloody brilliant programme.

In an instant, the Tour de France vanished from the agenda (it's basically just a foreign bike race, after all). They shuffled their chairs collectively closer towards him, angling them so that they wouldn't miss a word, while Brian Venner held court.

I could listen to Brian for hours. And I often do. I sat back and watched, enjoying the show.

* * *

The Show. Brian Venner's Show. That's what this is all about, in a roundabout way. From the lurid, mostly yellow, virtual cog-filled graphics of the title sequence, through the stage preview and news from the start line to the perfectly honed goodbye from the 'Master of Dry' Gary Imlach: that hour of July evenings, transfusing a massive intravenous hit of purest France into British living rooms; blasting blue-skied heat onto television screens only recently spattered with Wimbledon raindrops, the Tour has become, for some, compulsive viewing. It is, for those afflicted, a form of wildly addictive TV crack cocaine, with bicycles. And sometimes with other drugs, too.

Contrary to occasional popular belief, ITV are not daft. They don't do things for no reason, nor do they act simply out of the kindness of their hearts. They are not public service broadcasters. They have

no mandate to support minority sports. Shorn of
any income from subscriptions, or a licence fee, they
depend on viewers' numbers being sufficiently big to
justify an advertising spend.

Hence those irritating three-minute gaps when
you can dive off upstairs to have a pee. Your
pee breaks are how they stay alive (and I feed my
family, come to that). They will, in short, only invest
in anything where they see the potential for growth,
the potential of a return. And to give them credit,
this is a gig they've stuck with.

The reasons are obvious. In the years of my involvement (which, to put it bluntly, began with the
apotheosis of the Armstrong myth, endured the
turmoil of Landis, Rasmussen, Vinokourov and
Contador, and now encompass the Last Night Of
The Proms Tours, the Union Jack-waving Britfest it
has suddenly become), these years have seen expo-
nential growth in viewing figures.

In 2003, we were occasionally hard pushed to
scrape together a six-figure audience of any descrip-
tion. Nowadays, they push up to and over the critical
one million mark. That's almost a ten-fold increase
in as many years.

Here's the strange thing: I've never seen the
show. I only discovered it at precisely the same time I
started working on it.

I'm often asked what my perfect Tour de France
would be, and I can say (with only a small portion of

disingenuousness) that it would be to come home from work, pour a glass of wine, and sit down in front of the telly in time for the highlights show to start. I'd nip back out to the kitchen during the ad breaks to get crisps and nonsense like that. I wonder what experiencing the Tour like that would be like. Pretty enjoyable, I reckon.

It's an odd quirk of fate that I am uniquely unqualified to talk about our Tour de France coverage. I am conscious that there will be many people reading this who have seen it often, yearly, even religiously. I am equally well aware that there is a strong faction of the cycling community which will watch the free-to-air coverage only in extremis. These are people for whom Eurosport's offering gets closer to the race, and who dislike with a passion the amount of time (it's actually not a huge amount) we dedicate to content 'away' from the racing: Gary Imlach's editorials, my reports, Chris Boardman's analysis. This is a perfectly reasonable position. Our job, as much as it is to cater to the needs of the initiated, is to draw in passers-by, to make accessible the incomprehensible. We are a starting point for many, and sometimes people never move on. This is about the institution which Brian Venner and others have brought to British screens, through which a generation or two of Tour obsessives have first learned about cycling.

But first and foremost it's about a quintessential Englishman from the home counties, called Brian.

The year was 1948.

'I don't know why, but I became keen on broadcasting. And radio was the thing then.'

Brian Venner, reclining opposite me in a plush armchair at the sumptuous RAC Club in Pall Mall, a brandy in one hand, remembers how his school athletic team would compete against their local rivals.

Instead of taking part, instead of leaping into the sandpit, legs akimbo, or dashing through the white tape first on the grassy track, a young Brian Venner would be stalking the perimeter of the field with a huge infantry-style radio transmitter strapped to his back and a full set of Bakelite headphones balanced precariously across his head. He'd be 'broadcasting' the athletics, although to whom he was broadcasting was not entirely clear.

'I remember the warden of the school coming up to me and saying, "Who do you think you are? Barrington Dalby?"'

Brian chuckles happily at this recollection, which leaves me wondering who on earth Barrington Dalby was (he was, in fact, a former boxing referee who used to provide the expert analysis for the great Raymond Glendenning). I could imagine him grinning impishly at his teacher, before turning away and stumbling back towards the track, half buckling under the over-proportioned cast-iron weight of the field transmitter.

He went to Oxford to study engineering,

although he modestly claims he only got a place at St Edmund's Hall because they were desperate for any kind of sporting success, and Brian was small enough to pass muster as a cox.

'At that time, if you were tiddlywinks champion, they would have decided to take you. If you were any good at any sport at all, you were in.'

On the other hand, at Oxford, an undistinguished academic career was offset by the fulfillment of one significant sporting ambition. He won a Full Blue when he coxed the Oxford crew to a narrow defeat in the 1956 Boat Race. But that defeat inadvertently opened the door to Brian Venner's television career. Everything he has achieved in broadcasting, including the more than 30 years of televising the Tour, stems from those chilly 20 minutes on the Thames.

Some time later, he was invited to 'audition' at the BBC for the role of 'colour commentator' on their annual Boat Race coverage, to work alongside the great John Snagge (the stalwart who had commentated on the Coronation of King George VI and the Normandy landings, and other such trivialities). They sat Brian in what was quaintly known as a film theatre, thrust a lip mic into his hand, and told him to start talking in his own time.

A silent, flickering, out-of-focus replay of the previous year's Boat Race jumped into life on the screen in front of him. To his delight, he realised he was watching the 1956 edition, the one he had coxed.

No one at the BBC realised that he was commentating on a race he had been a part of.

'I knew every eddy of the river, I knew fucking everything. I gave it all this stuff about "brilliant coxing by Oxford!" And no one realised that it was me that I was talking about!'

He got the job, and in so doing saw off a formidable challenge from a gentleman called Sir Herbert Thompson, a BBC grandee in his late 60s who spoke only with a terrible stutter. Brian prevailed. Now he was up and running.

His languid home-counties tones graced the airwaves for three Boat Races in total. By the time of his third race, he'd become the 'lead commentator' (think Phil Liggett to someone else's Paul Sherwen). He was paired that year with a big, big radio star: Winford Vaughan Thomas. The legendary Welshman had made his name during World War Two for a report filed from an RAF Lancaster bomber, engaged in a night-time bombing raid over Berlin. But even that couldn't prepare him for working with Brian Venner, whose sense of mischief was blossoming.

Vaughan Thomas, a rowing novice, had asked Brian to give him something to say, so that he sounded like he knew what he was talking about. This, in the smoke-and-mirrors world of broadcasting is still a surprisingly common practice. Brian thought about what he could offer Vaughan Thomas, and then told him that, as the race approached Hammersmith

Bridge, he'd normally expect Cambridge to 'put in a bit of a spurt'. Vaughan Thomas was delighted with this nugget, and the plan was hatched that, as the bridge approached, Brian would pass over to his co-commentator to deliver it.

That's not quite what happened, though. As Hammersmith Bridge's ornate iron frame hove into view, he could see Vaughan Thomas at his side, twitching, and signalling that he should pass over the shared lip mic so that he might utter his killer line.

But Brian had torn up the script.

'I don't know why I said it.' Just as the two crews were passing under the bridge he exclaimed: 'This is where Cambridge traditionally put on a spurt.'

And with that he handed Vaughan Thomas the mic. The great Welshman looked aghast. He had nothing to say. 'I'd completely fucked him,' Brian remembers, half a century later, with a furious fit of schoolboy laughter.

Raymond Glendenning, the iconic voice of boxing commentary on the radio, didn't fare much better when paired with Brian either. He was, according to Brian, 'famous for lying', and was caught out by the advent of television, when everyone could see for their own eyes the nonsense he was talking. In the end, Brian tells me, he was a virtual derelict.

'Poor old Raymond, who'd been a household name, reduced to going round boxing halls bumming gin and tonics off people.'

By now Brian was established as something of an all-rounder at the BBC. Not only was he a master engineer, involved in the technical direction of the very first satellite broadcasts from Telstar, he also directed the Apollo moon landings, the Silver Jubilee and several General Elections. Not a bad CV. But Grandstand was his main job, where he worked on more World Cups and Olympic Games than he can remember. But he also kept an editorial finger in the pie. In fact, he remembers how he gave Football Focus its name. That's a show that's still running now, more than 40 years later.

In fact, if, like me, you were weaned in nylon-curtained front rooms on BBC Sport's output in the 1970s, you probably didn't realise that you were being introduced to the flickering wider world by none other than Brian Venner. He seemed to be involved in almost everything: the Where's Wally? of black-and-white (and latterly technicolour) television.

In 1978, after clandestine meetings in the Grosvenor House hotel, he was head-hunted by the US sports agent Mark McCormack, and his TV production company TWI. He played hardball for while, but, in the end, he took their dollar.

'They tried to fob me off with a Mini, but I got an Alfa Romeo instead.'

His first duties at TWI, who had contracts to produce content for BBC Sport, was to overhaul their fledgling coverage of *Superstars*.

'TWI had been taking money for doing fuck-all. It was all amateur nonsense. I took it up, and produced it properly for the first time. It was tinpot before that. I stirred it all up, because I knew people like Ron Pickering and David Vine.'

And if *Superstars* now knew the 'Venner Effect', then it wasn't long before cycling, and the Tour de France, would come to experience it, too.

* * *

A diversion: I once got talking to Chris Boardman about *Superstars*.

The span of his career neatly sidestepped the iconic crossover sport show, which meant that he was never called upon to line up for the pole vault alongside Paul Gascoigne. It had finally died a temporary death in 1985. But, when the format sputtered back to British TV screens some ten years ago, Boardman was ripe for the picking. He had finished riding, and hadn't yet cemented his current status as The Richest Man In Halfords, so this fell just nicely. He needed a target to aim at.

He started running. He grew a beard. He got fast, strong, supple. He took it absurdly seriously, demanding to see the rules and regulations ahead of time. It was a rabid attention to detail, of course, that won him so much during his racing career. And it was the same application of marginal gains that led to him establishing a revolutionary new way of executing the squat thrust, the blue-riband event of *Superstars*.

He noticed there was no rule that stipulated the need to 'jump' the legs forward and back. You could, it seemed, slide. In fact, you could slide in precisely the same way that Brian Jacks slid to success all the late 1970s. At the time, it had seemed borderline unethical, and the organisation had had to clamp down on it. Now, Boardman was at it again. And, once again, the organisers had been caught napping.

So, having sought reassurance that the venue had a polished wooden floor, he invested in the right pair of socks, with just enough 'slidiness' to shuttle his legs back and forth at bewildering speed.

'I smashed it,' he tells me, not without pride. But sadly it wasn't enough to win the overall competition. And when the event was re-staged the next year, in a bizarre echo of his cycling career, they'd rewritten the rule book, and redefined the shape of the squat thrust, forever.

Shame.

* * *

Back at the RAC club, Brian has finally got to the point in his story where he is brought face to face with the Tour de France.

It was 1980, the year of Joop Zoetemelk. The year

in which British television, in the country-club shape
of *Superstars'* Brian Venner, first sat up and started
to pay attention to the great race. It would still be
several years before it made it onto our screens (apart
from ITV's 20-minute round-ups of the whole race
on World Of Sport), but this was the start of it all.
And who knows what might have happened, or not
happened, had Brian Venner not been sent abroad?

He was parachuted into France on a semi-
secretive mission. Obviously, he wasn't literally parachuted, although ASO have always believed in the
power of glamorous forms of air travel to impress
TV executives. They tend to pick them up from Le
Bourget airport in Paris in a fleet of choppers, which
take off simultaneously, noses dipped to the tarmac,
just because it looks cool.

Not long after arriving at the start of the penultimate stage in Auxerre, he found himself whisked
to the front of the race, sharing the back seat of the
lead car with the race director Félix Lévitan, who had
been flirting with McCormack's dollars.

The preposterous, and still unrealised, dream was
to take the *Grand Départ* to Manhattan. Brian Venner's
fact-finding trip to France was the first move on the
chess board, making him the pawn in the passenger
seat. It was also his first experience of any kind of
bike race. Lévitan, the autocrat, put on a show that
was designed to impress the easily impressionable
'*homme de* McCormack'.

He called up the helicopter pilot, who buzzed the car and dipped his rotor blades in greeting. He jumped up and down, poking his imperiously-sized nose out of the sunroof, and shrieking '*En avant! En avant!*' to everyone and no one in particular. Brian was thrilled, not least with the Champagne on offer in a cool-box.

When, passing through some anonymous little town, the local mayor had the temerity to pull out ahead of the race in his mayoral limousine, the full brunt of Lévitan's *force majeure* was brought to bear on him. At once, the offending vehicle was surrounded by motorbike outriders seconded from the Presidential Guard (Mitterand's very own). The interloper was forced unceremoniously off the route.

'He was a real *Gauleiter*,' remembers Brian, in open-mouthed admiration.

This was a Boy's Own adventure. The actual stage (from Auxerre to Fontenay-sous-Bois) was won by Sean Kelly, but none of that was of any great interest. What had most beguiled Brian Venner had been the sight of the property tycoon Guy Merlin, whose eponymous company sponsored the Tour de France, biting the cap off a beer bottle in a school hall which had been commandeered for hospitality.

The visit had been a success. Not because the Tour ever ended up in Manhattan, but because it had ignited something in Brian Venner, which, after smouldering away for a few more years, would lead inevitably to the Tour reaching the population of the British Isles for the first time in 1986. And we all know where that would ultimately lead.

* * *

Without the birth of Channel Four, perhaps none of this would have happened. As the fresh, new, alternatively minded face of British television, they needed to nurture sports that they could call their own. They also had a mandate, which discouraged the mainstream, and, by necessity, zoomed in on minority interest. And, at the time, there was no doubting that cycling was right up there in the public consciousness with clay-pigeon shooting and Kabaddi. Tiny.

First of all, city-centre cycling was trialled. Alan Rushton (an erstwhile colleague of the current Tour of Britain race director Mick Bennett) had come along with the concept. He had the idea of coning off a lane for the TV motorbike. It seemed like a good idea at the time, but, actually, it didn't work.

'So I took it up, and eventually decided to get rid of all those fucking cones,' says Brian. 'They were just in the way. Just let the cameraman fight for himself on the course. People were highly impressed. It was a new thing.'

Adrian Metcalfe, the former Olympic silver-medal-winning 400-metre runner, was head of Channel Four Sport. He would later go on to head up

Eurosport, when it launched, where he would instantly latch onto cycling. But, at Channel Four, he was the first man to acquire the rights to the Tour de France and schedule a 30-minute nightly highlights show. It was 1986.

Brian Venner produced it. Richard Keys (who would go on to become the face of football on Sky Sports for the best part of 20 years, before his embarrassing exit) was hired as the anchorman.

'We presented it from the front window of Channel Four's offices, so that people walking past on the street could see Richard Keys talking to the camera, etc. It was a gimmick.'

A gimmick, maybe, but it gained an instant, and unflinchingly loyal, audience. It was compelling viewing. Not always for the obvious reasons.

'Richard Keys had a very hairy chest. He wore an open-necked shirt, and the hairs would be crawling over the collar. He was eventually criticised by somebody in the public for looking like "an exploding mattress", which I thought was quite fun.'

Then there was Phil Liggett. If Keys' tenure was restricted to a handful of Tours, Liggett's has been considerably longer. And he was there from the very start. Brian recalls their first conversation: 'I rang him up and told him what we were going to do, and I said to him, "Please will you come and be the commentator, because I am told we've got to use you."'

Typical Venner bluster: charming and belligerent

in equal measure. But Liggett's voice has been ever present, since that moment.

* * *

Let's deal with this matter, before we proceed.

Phil Liggett has enjoyed better years, of that there is no doubt. It's clear enough that his association (it has been a friendship, in the past) with Lance Armstrong has led him to take a position that has dented his reputation in the eyes of many. The criticism that has come his way has not been entirely unexpected, given his profile, and the nature of his public utterances. Look at the evidence, weigh up his words. I will not do that for you.

The media landscape is broad and varied. Each publication, each outlet, each journalist or broadcaster services a separate need, and answers to a subtly different mandate. Televising a live race, which is where Phil Liggett has made his name, is primarily about just that: televising a race. The voice of the commentator is the accompaniment to the action, to spot the names we might otherwise miss, fill in the gaps which we may not even know are there, and to reflect (and augment) our own thrill at the spectacle. It is there, after all, to thrill. Cycling is, broadly speaking, entertainment.

The wider context, the ethics, the feuds, the pacts, the doping, those things of fundamental importance to the individual fates of the protagonists and the future credibility of the spectacle? These things are of great significance. But, for the few seconds in which an athlete, any athlete, corrupt or pure, is blasting clear to win, the race is all that matters.

And it is only a few seconds; a life-affirming, temporary suspension of disbelief. Because the moment the rider eases up and coasts to a standstill, taking the win, and lapping up the adulation and congratulation, is the moment at which the questioning comes rushing back in to fill the void.

That is where Gary Imlach's raised eyebrow can act as shorthand for doubt, and at the other end of the spectrum, Paul Kimmage can fire off his salvoes. That's where I stick my microphone in. How the rest of the media react is key. But the TV commentator should stand apart. His role is different.

Those are the precious seconds when the accelerating cadence of the race finds its mirror image in Liggett's rising intonation. There is, to my mind, not one commentator out there who can match him when it comes to calling a finish. It is a great skill. And that is probably why Phil Liggett is about to embark on his 41st Tour de France. Everything else is surplus to requirement. Perhaps you've already made up your minds.

For many people, Phil Liggett's defining moment came in 1987, on a fog-bound mountain, with Pedro Delgado looking to cement his victory.

'The helicopters were grounded.' Brian recalls the near impossibility of following the race that day. 'We only had Moto One via a plane – that was the only camera going. So we're just looking at Delgado. We didn't know where Roche was. Liggett's commentating as best as he can. The cars keep coming in, and suddenly he's spotted someone.

That looks like Roche. That looks like Stephen Roche! It's Stephen Roche!

'He collapsed, as it happened, right under Liggett's commentary box. So he's leaning out, looking down, and there's Roche. And eventually, he can get the mic down to him, and get a gasp from Roche.'

That kind of broadcasting – ad hoc, chaotic, improvised, and almost wholly unpredictable – is what makes the Tour de France fantastically different. It's still a memory which needs toasting, so Brian Venner takes a warming sip of brandy and sits back.

'I thought that was fantastic!'

'Being there' was clearly everything.

By the end of the 1980s, Channel Four's Tour coverage took the big step forward. It crossed the over the water and actually went to France, leaving behind its shop window studio. It was an inevitable move. After Richard Keys, Phil Liggett was used as a presenter, as well as a commentator. He would stand, immaculately framed, his silvering hair neatly parted, microphone in hand, in front of the relevant finish line of the day, often with Paul Sherwen (only recently retired from cycling) as his wingman. And, at this time, Gary Imlach, whose background had been in news (as well as pioneering C4 coverage of American Football), came on board as a reporter.

In those days of limited, or non-existent, British success, Gary occasionally had the freedom to leave the race for days at a time so that he could film some wonderful travelogue pieces – some more surreal than others. Brian recalls every one.

'I remember him climbing up the inside of a statue of the Virgin Mary. There was a door that opened out of the Virgin Mary's navel, and Gary's face poked out. It was fantastic stuff.'

Despite the lack of British success, Channel Four paid £15,000 to put a motorbike in the race. Every morning, during the roll-out, they'd get a very special preview to the day's racing. Brian remembers how the Channel Four cameraman on the back of a bike would gravitate to the same rider every day.

'We had a close association with Allan Peiper. He'd do a piece for us every day on the roll-out. He'd tell us what was going to happen, and what the tactics were.'

The cameraman was Glenn Wilkinson, who I worked with during my first two Tours. Glenn died very suddenly back in 2004, far too young. When he worked on the race, he provided Channel Four viewers with a unique perspective.

'Glenn would capture special shots of crashes. In

those days the French didn't have such an eye for detail; they weren't as good at picking things up as they are now,' says Brian.

And on one stage in particular – on the Champs-Élysées at the final time trial of the 1989 Tour – he was right there where it mattered, when it mattered. The extra camera came into its own. French TV had entirely missed the story of the Tour.

'The shots we got of Greg LeMond watching and waiting to see whether Laurent Fignon would beat his time… The look on his face, and then leaping up in the air when he realised he'd won… That was all our camera, our bike camera. That was one of my great memories, those shots of LeMond.'

The Tour continually threw up unexpected situations for a production crew from the UK, unschooled in bike racing. It was, necessarily, determinedly, different. On one occasion, Glenn and his moto pilot slid off the road in the wet, and into the crowd, buckling a bystander's bike. They were almost lynched. Instead of a beating, Glenn was 'arrested' by the crowd, while the moto pilot had to drive to the finish and return with cash to pay for the damages before they would release him.

And then there was the time that they ignored a gendarme's red bat, ducked under it, and rode on. They were summarily thrown off the race. This incensed the commercially-minded Brian Venner.

'I rang them up, and mentioned the money and

the contract and said, "Can I have my money back?" It was almost as if the colour drained from their faces. They couldn't believe it, really. It was almost as if they'd never thought of that. And so we were given a final warning, and our bike was back in the race.'

The show grew steadily during the sporadically successful 'Boardman years', and despite the monotony of the Indurain wins. For Channel Four, still very much fighting for viewers as a minority station, audiences of 700,000 to 800,000 were rewarding.

But then came the ominous thwack of leather and willow: cricket sounded the death knell for the Tour de France. In 2001, Channel Four's move into the national summer sport knocked cycling off the schedules. They had no room for it anymore, and reluctantly ceded the rights, allowing Brian Venner to take them to whomever might decide to show the race, which, production costs aside, were now being passed on, effectively, for free. It has to be admitted, the queue was not especially long.

That year, the ill-fated ITV Sport Channel launched, broadcast exclusively on the even-more-ill-fated ITV Digital platform, with their reliably funny Johnny Vegas-with-the-monkey ad campaign, and appallingly unreliable technology.

They mostly showed football (I know, because I used to present a weekly show for them). But in order to fill their schedules for the football-less month of July, they needed something continuous, long-winded and free. They scratched their chins and wondered. Brian had the answer. The Tour came to ITV.

And so it began again. I joined a couple of years later and, a decade on, I'm still at it. Even though a sizeable proportion of our viewership still think they're watching Channel Four, they haven't been for a long, long time.

Successive Directors of Sport at ITV have re-signed the rights over and over again. I once asked one of them – Brian Barwick – how much he had to pay ASO for a five-year contract.

'That's for me to know, Ned,' he told me. 'And for you to fuck off about.' Commercial sensitivities, I guess. Or maybe he just didn't like me much.

What of the future? Who knows? It may not last forever. Sky may prise away rights, and decide they want to own the Tour, lock, stock and bottom bracket. That is out of our hands. We just do the show.

How has the programme evolved in my (short) memory of it? A great deal (Boardman's joined the team), and not even slightly (Phil and Paul still call the race). Both of these assertions are true.

Brian knits his brow.

'I do worry about the balance between offering serious insight and entertaining an audience.'

Then he gets animated.

'I hate people coming along and trying to do "clever-clever" items about the sport, where it's a triumph of style over content. I hate that.'

He pauses to consider again.

'But on the other hand I'm not saying there isn't something in it. Maybe we need to relax a little. We've got some extremely professional guys.'

Change? We have dropped the little snatched pieces of riders talking to the camera in foreign languages in and out of commercial breaks. This is because they no longer have to traipse through a medical inspection before the Tour, so we can no longer ambush them individually on their way out.

Another change? We broadcast live every day. This was unimaginable a few years ago, when there was serious doubt as to whether enough people would find ITV4 on the dial of an afternoon (when they should be working) to justify the extra expense. But the viewing figures have exceeded expectations.

But that's about it. The rest has been pretty unaltered. In fact, there is not one show on British TV that has evolved less, I suspect. And that includes *The Antiques Roadshow*. In a race that .changes, the show remains constant.

And Brian? He continues to adore the sport. These days, he does as much as his age allows him on the production, based at the London HQ, which stitches the show together. His son James has taken over the more day-to-day management of things back at base. These are heady days for the Tour in the UK.

'When I was a kid I had a Raleigh Roadster. We used to ride a hundred miles a day. We thought we had to do a hundred miles a day, going from youth hostel to youth hostel. Every kid's got a bike, haven't they, more or less? Why hasn't it been a bigger sport in this country?

'Now, but only now, is it just beginning to build up to "really quite something". I like to think that we, on TV, have also had a big effect.'

We are reaching the end of our time together at the RAC Club. Brian glances at his watch from time to time. Any minute now, he is expecting Phil Liggett to arrive, and to accompany him to a wine tasting. They are old friends, with a shared history.

'I'm extremely proud of cycling. I feel I've been involved. I've published the sport on the TV, and God knows why it wasn't there before. I think I've had quite a say in building up cycling to be a great sport,' says Brian.

True, I find myself thinking, true. But that's not to forget *Superstars*.

I shake him by the hand.

'See you in the summer, Brian.'

Ned Boulting started his broadcasting career at Sky Sports, before moving to ITV. He has covered two football World Cups and loads of other stuff including the game of the Gods: darts. Over the last ten years he's been dabbling, and falling in love with, cycling. In 2013, he will cover the Tour de France for the 11th time. He lives in Lewisham, because he loves it there. Oh, and he's written a couple of books, too: *How I Won The Yellow Jumper* and *On The Road Bike: The Search For a Nation's Cycling Soul.*

3

Richard Williams recalls the grace of Charly Gaul, the climber from Luxembourg who won the Tour in 1958.

It wasn't Gaul's results but his daring exploits in the mountains that captured the imagination.

He personified panache in a way the metronomic efficiency of his rival Jacques Anquetil never could.

THE ANGEL OF THE MOUNTAINS

BY RICHARD WILLIAMS

When we're young, we don't always choose our heroes. Sometimes they seem to choose us. They just appear, as if out of nowhere, and attach themselves to us, their attributes fitting our emerging instincts and preferences. That's how, when I was on the verge of my teenage years, Charly Gaul became my first Tour de France hero.

Of course, I never saw him actually ride during those years. The only people whose riding I witnessed at first hand were competing in the Sunday-morning time trials along the local bypass, a few miles east of Nottingham. I did my paper round, then rode out to watch them.

Nor was there any international cycling to be seen on television at the end of the 1950s. The only images were those to be found in the black-and-white pages of the cycling magazines. So although I knew what Charly Gaul looked like, I could never become familiar with his style of pedalling. I didn't even know the colours of his jersey.

As a child I had liked Reg Harris in the way I

liked Stanley Matthews, Denis Compton, Don
Cockell or Stirling Moss: they were our first post-war
British sporting heroes, their exploits and attributes
celebrated in the pages of the *Eagle*. Reg rode a locally-
built Raleigh, too (or at least that's what the head-
badge and the lettering on the downtube claimed).
But there was something missing, and it wasn't just
that his exploits were confined to the track.

The enthusiasm for cycling evolved, like a parallel
interest in modern jazz, in almost complete isolation.
I wasn't a member of a cycling club, and having a
friend whose Claud Butler Coureur was equipped
with Weinmann brakes and Simplex gears was as
close as I came in those years to getting my hands on
a decent bike. But what I already knew was that the
word 'Continental' evoked a magical exoticism.

In cycling, anything Continental was preferable to
just about anything British. In that way, cycling was
similar to early rock and roll. Elvis Presley, Chuck
Berry, Fats Domino, Buddy Holly and the Everly
Brothers were the real thing: they were the musical
equivalents of Gino Bartali, Fausto Coppi, Hugo
Koblet, Jean Stablinksi and the *frères* Bobet. Our
home-grown pedallers were the equivalents of Cliff
Richard, Marty Wilde, Vince Eager, Billy Fury and
the King Brothers: dedicated and enthusiastic, and
not without talent or appeal, but hardly in the same
league. For all the brave efforts of Brian Robinson
and one or two others, not until the arrival of Tom

Simpson – our local boy, raised amid the North Notts coalfields – did it feel as though we had a performer worthy of mention in the same breath as the foreign stars.

When it came to the business of choosing a foreign hero, I nearly opted for Rik van Looy. Maybe it was his name, which in itself carried the suggestion of speed. But Van Looy, a one-day man without compare (still the only rider whose *palmarès* include Milan-San Remo, Flèche Wallonne, the Tour of Lombardy, Liège-Bastogne-Liège, Paris-Brussels, the Tour of Flanders, Ghent-Wevelgem, Paris-Roubaix and the road world championships), was primarily a great *rouleur* with a fantastic sprint, honed during his equally distinguished career on the track.

He surprised everyone when he copped the king of the mountains jersey in the 1960 Giro d'Italia by amassing enough points on the smaller climbs early in the race to see him through to Milan, and he pulled off what was generally acknowledged to be a fantastic ride over the Stelvio the following year. He was as good as it gets. But somehow, at least for my purposes, he lacked the necessary charisma.

Most of my generation opted for Jacques Anquetil, the smooth blond stylist who was 22 years old and doing his national service when he broke Coppi's hour record in 1956, and won the first of his five Tours de France a year later. In terms of dominating his era, he was the equivalent of Formula

One's Juan Manuel Fangio. The way he rode made
Maître Jacques, as he came to be known, a useful model
for every boy who ever slid his cycling shoes into a
pair of toe-clips; he had also developed a colourful
private life, although we were not to know that at the
time. For me, though, he simply won too often, and
not in a particularly interesting way.

Charly Gaul captured only a fraction of the prizes
that went the way of Van Looy and Anquetil, but he
had the combination of qualities that won my heart.
He was a climber, for a start, and climbers often get
the best nicknames. Federico Bahamontes, Gaul's
rival, was the Eagle of Toledo, which was pretty fine,
but to be known as the Angel of the Mountains was
simply unbeatable.

His given name was pretty good, too: trisyllabic,
with a natural fall of stress, short-short-long, what
poets would call an anapaest. 'Charly' was a world
away from the home-grown Charlies, and 'Gaul'
made him sound French, which I assumed he was
until I learnt that he came from the same place as
Radio Luxembourg, which brought the sounds of
Elvis, Chuck, Fats, Buddy and the Evs crackling into
a British boy's bedroom on a wavering medium-wave
signal from the distant principality. That was another
reason for liking him.

Then there was the way Charly Gaul looked on a
bike. At that time I had no way of knowing that while
climbing he favoured small gears, pedalling smoothly

at a high cadence in a way that would become more or less standard practice almost half a century after his prime.

Even in a photograph, he didn't have the air of someone who ground uphill through strength alone. There was something about the way he looked in the pages of the magazines, a slender figure – 1.73 metres tall, 63 kilograms in weight – radiating a certain grace in the saddle. He was like Neil Harvey, the wonderful left-handed batsman of Australia's 1950s cricket team, or Alfredo di Stefano, the Argentinian maestro who ran the great Real Madrid side: each of them had a frictionless quality – handy for an off-drive or a defence-splitting pass, certainly, but particularly useful to a cyclist.

Facially, too, Charly Gaul had something special. If cycling had a James Dean, he was the man. His features suggested sensitivity, possibly introversion, even unknowability: he fitted the mould of the emerging post-war protagonists of novels by Albert Camus and films by Michelangelo Antonioni. Men portrayed by Marcello Mastroianni and Alain Delon, whose effortless elegance failed to cloak an existential alienation from the world around them. Or, in my beloved modern jazz, the trumpeters Miles Davis and Chet Baker, who produced a soundtrack to introspection. If there was something romantic about how Charly Gaul looked, the same could certainly be said for the way he rode.

His finest accomplishments were acts of drama, of self-realisation, played out not amid the heat and noise of a velodrome or over the bone-rattling cobbles of a Flandrian Classic but on the most spectacular stage cycling has to offer, the high mountains, where angels and eagles could do battle as they soared towards the heavens.

* * *

Gaul was born in Pfaffenthal, in the city of Luxembourg, on December 8, 1932. He worked in a butcher's shop and as a slaughterman in the abattoir of nearby Bettembourg while establishing his reputation as an amateur racer. (Had he been a different type of racer, perhaps he would have become known as the Butcher.)

Cyclo-cross was an early speciality, his prowess at the winter sport giving an indication of what would become one of his defining characteristics: an ability to plough through rain and snow to win races in conditions that others found discouraging. By the time he turned professional at the age of 20, his amateur record included 60 race wins in four years, including a stage win up the Grossglockner pass during the Tour of Austria, breaking the record for the climb while riding through a thunderstorm.

Terrot-Hutchinson was his first team, and he stayed with them for two seasons. Second place in the Critérium du Dauphiné Libéré in 1953, behind Lucien Teisseire, was followed a year later by a win in the Circuit des Six Provinces and third in the world championships in Solingen, behind Louison Bobet and Fritz Schär. He rode the Tour de France in both years with the Luxembourg team, failing to finish on either occasion, but that win in the Six Provinces, which included a prodigious climb of the snow-covered Galibier in sub-zero temperatures, had marked him out for further attention.

He spent the 1955 season with another French trade team, Magnat-Debon, but it was back in his country's jersey that he made his first impact on the Tour. A majestic breakaway on the stage from Thonon-les-Bains to Briançon, in which he had a lead of five minutes going over the Col de Télégraphe and almost 15 minutes at the top of the Galibier, was followed by a second stage victory in Saint-Gaudens, and eventually by third place on the podium in Paris, behind Louison Bobet and Jean Brankart, and the king of the mountains prize.

Then came the switch to the team in whose jersey his first great triumph was achieved: Faema-Guerra, jointly sponsored by a Milanese manufacturer of espresso machines and the makers of bicycles carrying the name of Learco Guerra, a Giro winner and world champion in the 1930s, known in his racing days as The Human Locomotive. Guerra was now the team manager, assisted by Guillaume

Driessens, later to be Eddy Merckx's *directeur
sportif* at Faemino and Molteni.

Gaul's team-mates that first year included
Bahamontes and Van Looy; he was accompanied by
two fellow Luxembourg riders, Marcel Ernzer and
Willy Kemp, both older than him by half a dozen
years. Ernzer was his devoted personal *domestique*;
Kemp, a former team-mate at Terrot-Hutchinson,
had won a Tour stage the previous year, from Namur
to Metz.

As the 1956 Giro left Merano, a spa town in the
South Tyrol once favoured by Franz Kafka, and
headed for the Dolomites, Gaul lay 24th in the overall standings with three days to go, despite having
won a mountain stage from Pescara to Campobasso
at the end of the first week and a timed hill-climb in
Bologna at the end of the second.

While rivals fell away amid the snow, ice and a
storm that raged throughout the 242-kilometre stage,
dozens of them leaving the race altogether on the
final climb up the Monte Bondone, Gaul pedalled
his way to an historic win. Legend says that he was
revived halfway up the last ascent by Guerra, who
poured warm water over the rider's half-frozen body
and supervised a massage before sending him back
out to finish eight minutes ahead of his nearest pur-
suer and more than 12 minutes ahead of Fiorenzo
Magni, the defending champion. Two days later Gaul
rode into Milan in the *maglia rosa* and, with a margin

of three minutes and 27 seconds over Magni, accepted the first of his three grand tour victories.

There would be two stage wins in that year's Tour de France: the first in a 151-kilometre time trial beginning and ending on the undulating grand prix circuit of Les Essarts, outside Rouen, and the second in a classic 250-kilometre Alpine stage from Turin to Grenoble, including the Croix de Fer and the Luitel. But he finished 13th overall, more than half an hour behind the winner, Roger Walkowiak.

A year later, unable to repeat his victory in the Giro after a promising start, he helped Gastone Nencini beat Louison Bobet, whom he detested, not least because Bobet had attacked when Gaul stopped for a pee earlier in the race. Neither was there good fortune in that year's Tour, which exposed his vulnerability to high temperatures: the race began in Nantes, and a heatwave forced Gaul to retire after reaching Caen at the end of the second stage, leaving the 23-year-old Anquetil to take his first victory.

It was in 1958 that Charly overcame the inevitable weakness of his rag-bag Luxembourg-and-the-rest team to win the Tour, profiting from splits in the French camp and putting Anquetil on the back foot by winning a 46-kilometre time trial in freezing rain in Châteaulin at the start of the second week. There would be another victory in a *contre-la-montre* ten days later, this time over 21.5 kilometres from Bédoin to the summit of Mont Ventoux, and a

third over 74 kilometres from Besançon to Dijon on
the penultimate day.

The defining day of that Tour, however, came not
in the contests against the watch but on stage 21, over
a 219–kilometre *parcours* from Briançon to Aix-les-
Bains. The veteran Raphaël Géminiani, wearing the
yellow jersey, held an advantage of 16 minutes over
Gaul as they set off, the peloton ambling over the
Lautaret in acceptable conditions before the weather
closed in as they left Uriage-les-Bains on the steep,
twisting ascent to the Col de Luitel. So confident was
Gaul that he identified to Bobet the hairpin at which
he intended to make his attack.

As good as his word, he broke clear with
Bahamontes, dropping the Spaniard as he made the
bridge well before the 1,235m summit, clearing the
ski station at Chamrousse and soaring over the pass
in freezing rain, with the Porte, the Cucheron and the
Granier still to come.

Maintaining his rhythm while his rivals fell apart,
skimming past families who had left home hoping
for a picnic but now emerged shivering from their
Renault Dauphines and Citroën 2CVs to cheer his
appearance, he crossed the finish line in Bourget-en-
Aix to receive a kiss from the first Madame Gaul,
gamine and suitably trenchcoated, with a lead of 12
minutes over his nearest pursuers.

He had taken 15 minutes out of Géminiani,
while Anquetil, 22 minutes adrift, had contracted a

bronchial infection in the filthy conditions.

Two days later in Dijon, with Anquetil coughing blood, Gaul took the yellow jersey for the first time. In another 24 hours he would be riding into the Parc des Princes and mounting the top step of the podium, flanked by Vito Favero and Géminiani.

That was the last time he wore the *maillot jaune*. He won the Giro again in 1959, with the EMI-Guerra team, holding the pink jersey for 14 of the 22 stages and finishing six minutes ahead of Anquetil, with Diego Ronchini in third place.

Gaul won a stage to Grenoble in the 1959 Tour, and another in 1961, finishing third in Paris that year, behind Anquetil and Guido Carlesi, the Italian stealing second place in the closing metres of the sprint to the line in the Parc des Princes.

He raced unsuccessfully in the 1962 and 1963 editions, with Gazzola-Fiorelli and Peugeot-BP, and thereafter his decline was rapid. After a year with Lamot-Libertas, a Belgian team co-sponsored by a brewery and a cycle manufacturer, he left the sport at the end of 1965.

In retirement, he ran a café near Luxembourg's main railway station. But the failure of his second marriage and the lure of solitude led him to a hut in the Ardennes, where he spent the next decade and a half as a virtual hermit. Every summer, he said, he hooked up a portable TV to his car battery in order to watch the Tour.

Eventually he was coaxed back into the public eye. The Luxembourg government employed him in its sporting archives, he married for a third time, and he accepted invitations to visit the races in which he had made his reputation, sometimes accompanied by his daughter.

Dumpy, bespectacled, with a grey beard, wearing strangely assorted clothes, he had successfully erased all traces of the mountain angel of his youth, but in October 2002 he was among the former Tour winners invited to the presentation of the following year's centenary race, and in February 2004 he put on a suit to attend the funeral of Marco Pantani, whom he admired.

By the time he died from a lung infection on December 6, 2005, two days short of his 73rd birthday, he had been welcomed back into the sporting family of which his personality had made him so awkward a member.

Those who had watched him from a tent pitched next to a *Deux Chevaux* beside a rain-soaked mountain road in the Chartreuse, or had merely followed his progress in the pages of a weekly magazine, knew little of his unpredictability and his reclusive tendencies.

Anyway, that would have been beside the point. Charly Gaul didn't have a record to match that of Anquetil, but he gave us a vision of what cycling could be. And each year, sitting down to watch the

Tour, we hope to see him reincarnated as the road tilts upwards and some slight figure slips off the front of the peloton to dance the skies.

Richard Williams is a former chief sports writer of *The Guardian*, to which he now contributes a weekly column. He has covered six Olympic Games, five World Cups and many other major sporting events, including the Tour de France. His books include *The Death of Ayrton Senna* and *Enzo Ferrari: A Life*. He has also written extensively about music – his website is www.thebluemoment.com – and film. He spends too much time looking at his road bikes and not enough time riding them.

4

The arrival of the Colombians at the Tour in 1983 was a big step toward Félix Lévitan's goal of making the race a global event.

Though relatively inexperienced amateurs, the Colombian riders soon made their presence known.

Lucho Herrera won the country's first stage in 1984. Four years later Fabio Parra was third overall.

Klaus Bellon Gaitán charts the rise of cycling's popularity in Colombia and remembers when a nation had its collective ear glued to a radio listening to the Tour.

NERVOUS BUT PREPARED

BY KLAUS BELLON GAITÁN

By 1955, the populous metropolis of Bogotá bustled with activity. That, however, was not the case for 18 days in late May and early June. During those days, Colombia's capital city took on a different and curious character. The streets were eerily quiet, as the city centre's sidewalks remained deserted for hours, only occupied by a large number of bicycles, resting along the windows of cafés and restaurants.

In the late afternoon, the silence would suddenly break, as the live radio broadcast of that day's Vuelta a Colombia stage came to a close. Countless bodies emptied into the streets, many mounting their bikes and riding away maniacally. With the city's streets now teeming with bicycles, a young reporter from the Colombian daily *El Espectador* took notice.

Gabriel García Márquez, still decades away from winning the Nobel Prize in literature, was already a keen observer of Colombians and their many idiosyncrasies. He wrote an article for *El Espectador* on the flurry of cyclists in Bogotá's streets after each Vuelta stage. 'As the stage ends, these urban cyclists

– in a frenzy as a result of the exciting narrations of
the day's race on the radio – throw themselves onto
the street.'

Márquez observed that the countless cycling fans
who took to the roads appeared to be in an altered
state due to the excitement of the day's race. This was,
the young reporter concluded, a fever or an illness
that Colombians were suffering from, one for which
only cycling could be blamed. One of the country's
brightest minds had accurately diagnosed Colombia's
population: the entire mountainous South American
country was delirious with passion for cycling.

That feverish passion continued as the deeply
Catholic nation identified with the pain, suffering
and martyrdom that had always been inherent in
cycling – climbing in particular. But it would not be
until the 1980s that Colombia's unbridled passion for
the sport would be experienced at the highest level:
at the Tour de France.

The road to the Tour first led Colombians
through another French race: the Tour de l'Avenir.
It was there that Colombia's dreams of racing in the
largest stage race in the world truly began.

AN UNLIKELY REQUEST, AND AN UNLIKELY ANSWER

In early August of 1980, Hector Urrego, a Colombian journalist returning home from the Moscow
Olympics, stopped by the offices of *L'Equipe* in

Paris. He had secured a meeting with the organisers of the Tour de l'Avenir through contacts in the French press that he'd made during his time in the Soviet Union. Urrego's reason for wanting to meet was singular, though it was loaded with aspirational possibilities. Simply put, Urrego wanted to have a Colombian team compete in the Tour de l'Avenir, which was only four weeks away. To say this was a long shot would be an unbelievable understatement, but Urrego was hopeful. He thought that if nothing else, perhaps a seed could be planted to allow Colombia's diminutive climbers to compete in a future edition of the race.

Urrego, accompanied by two other Colombian journalists, explained the significance and validity of Colombian cycling, doing his best to get his point across in French. He was sure of the fact that the riders would be competitive and perhaps even win a major race such as the Tour de l'Avenir.

'At the time, I would have conversations with Raúl Mesa, who went on to be one of the most successful Colombian team directors, regarding the state of amateur cycling,' Urrego said. 'As we saw it, the sport at that level was dominated by the Soviets. In Europe, they were feared, but what people in Europe didn't know was that when the Soviets raced here in South America, in a race like Venezuela's Vuelta al Táchira, our riders were on par with them, and often beat them. So we figured that the same would be true in Europe, if only we could get Colombian riders over there.'

As optimistic as Urrego was while making his point, even he was surprised when an answer was given on the spot. Yes, he was told, a Colombian team could compete at the Tour de l'Avenir, since the Venezuelan squad had been forced to pull out at the last minute. Stunned, Urrego called Raúl Mesa in Colombia to give him the good news, but also to tell him that they would need to secure all the necessary funding for the team within 24 hours, since the race organisers wanted an answer quickly. Mesa complied, and managed to secure funding from Freskola, the soft drink company that sponsored the small trade team he ran.

As unlikely as their invitation to the race had appeared, a good performance seemed even more far-fetched to many within the sport. The team, however, managed to deliver, as Alfonso Flórez took the general classification, having managed to fend off numerous attacks from Sergei Soukhoroutchenkov, then the reigning Olympic road champion.

Upon returning home, the team was greeted by hundreds of thousands of well-wishers, who lined Bogotá's roads in order to catch a glimpse of the returning heroes. After nearly 30 years, the fever that Gabriel García Márquez spoke of had not subsided. In fact, the passion for the sport in Colombia had only increased.

After Flórez's win, European race organisers began to take notice of the Colombians – especially after strong showings in Switzerland, Italy and Spain. But a chance to compete at the Tour de France was still beyond reach, due to the organiser's insistence in only allowing professional trade teams into the race.

That would change in 1983.

NERVOUS, BUT WELL PREPARED

In 1983, race director Jacques Goddet chose to allow amateur national teams into the race, and an all-Colombian team lined up at the start of the Tour de France for the first time.

Having secured financial backing from the battery manufacturer Varta, the team's riders spent the month prior to the Tour visiting small corner stores throughout Colombia, giving away batteries as part of Varta's initial 35,000 peso (roughly £70,000 or $106,000 today) investment in the team.[1]

Once at the Tour, the all-amateur squad felt ill at ease. On the first day of the race, they looked around nervously as they prepared for the time trial at Fontenay-sous-Bois. Edgar 'Condorito' Corredor, only 20 years old at the time, was in awe as he walked by luminaries of the sport that he'd previously only seen in cycling magazines.

The Colombian cycling fan in him took over. He sought out a pen to get autographs from fellow

riders, but his more experienced team-mate, Patrocinio Jiménez, corrected him sternly. 'I told him,
"Don't be an asshole – they're no different from us,
and we can do everything they can do."'

Despite Jiménez's leadership, the nervous tension
among the Colombian riders remained.

'We didn't understand anything that was happening, and we were scared to death,' he said.

With all the anxious energy running through their
bodies, some of the riders had to urinate several
times before the time trial. They found a few plants
in what they thought was an out-of-the-way spot,
and proceeded to empty their bladders. They were
promptly fined 70 francs each as a result of their
infraction. The race hadn't even started, and they
were already behind.

Despite the fines and their trepidations, the
team's fighting spirit remained intact as they readied
for the race. It was this stubborn spirit that carried
them through the Tour, which turned out to be more
difficult than any of them originally anticipated.

Two time trials penalised the Colombians, as did
long stretches of cobblestones in early stages of the
race – a surface unlike any they had encountered back
home. They were demolished, and Tour de l'Avenir
winner Alfonso Flórez was forced to retire before
the Tour reached the first mountain stage although
others, like Patrocinio Jiménez, managed to stay in
the race.

ESCARABAJOS IN FRANCE

The *escarabajo* is a flying beetle and the nickname of Colombian climber Ramon Hoyos, winner of five editions of the Vuelta a Colombia. His smooth and stubborn climbing abilities reminded some of a beetle, with the nickname eventually spreading to encompass all Colombian climbers.

As the Colombian press saw it, the 1983 Tour de France would be the first time that European contenders would learn about the climbing abilities of the Colombian *escarabajos*. But, with team leader Flórez, easily the best climber in the squad, out of the race, it was unclear who among the Colombian riders would be able to compete with the world's best. As it turned out, it was Patrocinio Jiménez who took charge, having already led the team off the bike.

On stage ten, the native of Ramiriquí attacked along with Robert Millar, and they held a sizeable gap for much of the day. On the final descent to Luchon, Jiménez lost time, but still managed to take fourth on the day. More importantly, he earned the polka-dot jersey, making him the first Colombian ever to do so. Jiménez held on to the jersey for five days, and realised just how right he'd been when he'd told his team-mate Edgar Corredor that riders from well-funded European trade teams were no different from the Colombians. And the Colombians' results made that more apparent. Corredor and Jiménez

finished the Tour as the two highest placed in the
team – 16th and 17th, respectively – despite having
haemorrhaged time in the race's early flat stages.
For a team of unknown amateurs from a relatively
unknown country (particularly within the scope of
cycling), the race was considered a success. Quietly,
however, all those involved knew they were capable
of achieving a good bit more.

A WATCHFUL EYE OVER YOUR SHOULDER

As Jiménez, who now works as a driver for tourists
who stay in Bogotá's many high-end hotels, thinks
back to the 1983 Tour, he smiles broadly. The team
had been nervous at the start of the race, sure, but
they weren't completely inexperienced either. They
were capable and prepared, something he's quick to
point out.

The team was made up of riders who had raced
and won at a high level throughout Central and South
America before. They hadn't come out of nowhere,
as some suspected. Colombia's team may have been
made up of riders who were young amateurs on
paper, but their legs said otherwise. More importantly,
he adds, they all had plenty of *malicia indigena* – a term
that comes up often when you speak to riders and
staff from those early Colombian teams.

Translated literally, the term means 'indigenous
malice,' but this is misleading. No ill will or ac-

tual malice is involved. The term refers to a keen awareness of both circumstances and surroundings (similar to being street-wise) that is generally believed to be an innate part of Colombians regardless of skin colour or ethnic background. In the context of cycling, *malicia indigena* translates to not only believing, but also knowing, that other riders will surely want to attack you first, and behaving accordingly. As a result you must attack first, trust no one, and always keep a watchful eye over your shoulder. To Jiménez, this was part of the mental fortitude that Colombian riders brought with them to the Tour, along with their uncanny, altitude-fuelled ability to climb.

'We were all peasants. We had an insatiable hunger for winning, in part perhaps because it meant more to us. We needed to win. We were an amazing group, and we were willing to sacrifice everything.'

Today, little has changed. Speak to a Colombian professional, and you'll often hear references to the financial realities that inspired them to race, as well as the need to aid entire families. To say that this accounts for Colombia's success in cycling in its entirety is inaccurate, but ignoring its influence would be foolish.

Corey Shouse Tourino, associate professor of hispanic studies and the director of the Latino/ Latin American studies programme at the College of St Benedict and St John's University in Minnesota, USA, lived and studied in Colombia, and has

studied Colombia's cycling culture in particular.
Shouse Tourino believes that Colombia's financial
realities have indeed played a crucial role influencing
men like Jiménez to race a bike at all.

'Some of the reason why it was cycling, and not
another sport, that captivated Colombians has to do
with particular economic conditions. Certainly the
more wealthy countries in Latin America emulate the
United States and Europe in a more "upscale" manner than Colombia. Think Argentina and Venezuela:
they have had similar experiences with imported
sports that are strongly associated with modernisa-
tion and progress. Venezuela, with all of its oil and
Miami-dreaming, is a hotbed of baseball, and Argentina is a place where rugby, polo and motor racing
have bloomed. These can be pretty capital-intensive
sports to promote.'

Colombians, by comparison, took to the bike,
and men like Jiménez often used it as a simple means
of transportation for earning a living, something that
remains true for many throughout Colombia's countryside. Riding a bike is a necessity, not a hobby. It's
a simple action that isn't thought about, much in the
same way that other cultures don't put much thought
into other activities.

Shouse Tourino explains further: 'Cycling is a
deeply organic part of Colombian culture. Americans, however, ride bikes the same way they drink
wine: these are prosthetic acts that require special

gear and a "rarified air" of intention and pretension.
Cycling for many in the US is indeed enjoyable, but
artificial, not organic, like making a big fuss over
that "special bottle of fermented grape juice" that
Italians put on their tables every single afternoon
without thinking about it.'

BIG BUSINESS

Despite the financial and social hardships that
Colombian riders had overcome and continued to
live through, the 1983 Tour de France made it clear
that cycling meant big business in Colombia, particularly as the masses turned their attention to the daily
stages from start to finish.

While Varta's bill for sponsoring the team had
nearly doubled by the time the race was finished,
the investment paid off. In fact, its share in the
battery market in Colombia jumped by a staggering
11 per cent as virtually every Colombian learned the
company had underwritten the team. At a time when
transistor radios and battery usage was unusually
high in Colombia (especially in its rural countryside,
where workers were often out in the fields), 11 per
cent of the battery market translated into an impressive amount of money. Sadly, however, the team's
riders were thanked for this sudden rise in revenue by
simply having their lunch paid for in Paris at the end
of the race.[2] But the financial impact of the sport in

Colombia was not relegated to the battery market. For the first time in the Tour's history, every single stage in the race's 1983 edition was broadcast in its absolute entirety. Not in France, Belgium or Italy, but in Colombia.

As unusual as Hector Urrego's visit to *L'Equipe*'s offices in 1980 may have seemed then, making the case for a Colombian team to race at the Tour de l'Avenir had paid off. With an all-Colombian team at the Tour, RCN radio sent a crew of 12 broadcasters and technicians to cover every kilometre of every stage live in an attempt to satisfy the country's insatiable appetite for the sport. The following year, the number of Colombian journalists at the race grew as Caracol, a competing station, began broadcasting, and every major newspaper sent journalists as well.

Colombians became transfixed by the Tour de France, just as they had been transfixed by the Vuelta a Colombia back in 1955 when Gabriel García Márquez first noticed massive crowds empty into Bogotá's streets.

Eventually, live television broadcasts of the Tour de France became commonplace in Colombia, but even then radio reigned supreme since stages happened during Colombia's work day.

RCN and Caracol saw revenues rise as they both carried live accounts of the race throughout the country. To the millions in Colombia who listened attentively through the 1983 Tour de France, it was the tenacity, the spirit – and, yes, the *malicia indigina* of men like Patrocinio Jiménez – that kept them buying endless supplies of Varta batteries. But the tone and delivery of the radio broadcasters contributed greatly, thus playing an undeniable part in Colombia's golden age of cycling.

AS MANY COINS AS PHYSICALLY POSSIBLE

Much like the riders who made up that 1983 squad, the Colombian broadcasters who were sent to cover the race may have been nervous at first, but they weren't completely inexperienced either. They had covered races throughout South and Central America, and were well versed in the necessary technical aspects of broadcasting. But it was their passionate delivery, not their technical prowess, that made them as much a part of the Tour de France for Colombians as the riders.

Never ones to shy away from displaying emotion on the air, Colombia's commentators took to the Tour de France with gusto, excitedly relaying every detail to an attentive audience back home, and sometimes breaking down into unintelligible fits of tears due to the excitement of a Colombian's performance. It's something that long-time commentator Phil Liggett remembered well as he spoke to *Bicycling* magazine in 2012.

'When the Colombians came, they brought all the

big names – Luis Herrera and Fabio Parra. And the Colombian media came in full force as well, with TV, newspapers, and radio broadcasters… They would be commentating in a voice fit for a finishing sprint when the race had just left the start town.'

A report about Colombians at the Tour from French television in 1984 confirms this. As 'Lucho' Herrera came close to winning a hilly stage into Grenoble, one of Colombia's radio commentators can be seen crying uncontrollably as he screams at the top of his lungs, *'Viva Colombia! Viva Herrera!'*

Such displays were not uncommon. In fact, they were just one of the reasons why other commentators and journalists noticed their Colombian counterparts. 'These two Colombian radio broadcasters showed up with this cassette player with all of their advertising commercials loaded on a cassette tape,' Liggett remembered. 'We'd see them trading their French francs for a bunch of coins, and they would run a one-hour radio program back to Bogotá over payphones. They would be pumping coins into this pay phone and yelling into the phone, and then every now and again throw on the cassette tape for a commercial break.'

According to Hector Urrego, who was one of the commentators with a cassette player and massive amounts of coins, Liggett remembers correctly.

'During that first Tour in 1983, we simply didn't have all the necessary technical equipment. As such, one of our primary jobs every day during that first Tour de France was to find a bank, and get as many coins as physically possible. We'd then find a payphone, and make our calls back to Colombia, which of course were costly and often very long. Because of this, our cars at the Tour were absolutely loaded with coins.'

But the phones that Colombia's radio pioneers used weren't always public ones. Even today, Urrego laughs in disbelief as he remembers one particular incident during the 1983 Tour.

'In one stage, we lost the aerial signal from the car during the broadcast. We were scrambling, because we knew how many people were listening back in Colombia. We stopped in this small town, and found a small Catholic seminary. This kind, old priest graciously allowed us to use his phone so we could make a call, which he believed was only to Paris.

'Little did he know! Of course, we were calling all the way to Colombia, and the call lasted over an hour. On our way out, I gave him the equivalent of maybe one hundred dollars or more in charity for their parish, which was a good bit of money then. The elderly priest asked why I was being so generous, and I told him it was just charity, but he'd find out what it was for soon enough!'

Such were the lengths to which Colombian commentators went. While emotional broadcasts and coin-fuelled reports may have aroused interest among the international press, it's imperative that one keeps in mind the significance that these broadcasts had to Colombians back home.

'Most historians talk about Colombia as a nation of regions,' explains Corey Shouse Tourino. 'And Jesus Martin Barbero [a Colombian philosopher, anthropologist and semiotician] goes as far as arguing that it remained a nation of nations until radio broadcasts united Colombians with a shared, invisible sense of belonging to a shared space and culture... Given that cycling was both the most important sport and national spectacle – at least of a positive and popular nature – first the Vuelta and the Clásico RCN, and later the Tour, the Giro and the Vuelta a España were essential to convincing Colombians that Colombia existed as a singular concept that was worth defending and celebrating at home [and] on the world stage.'

Hector Urrego concurs. He says part of the reason cycling is such an integral part of Colombian culture is because it taught its citizens about themselves, and what they were capable of. But perhaps more importantly, it taught them about their own country and its geography.

In doing so, cycling became a mental and social meeting point of sorts – the first of its kind for the South American country. The meaning of the sport only grew as Colombians began to race in the Tour de France.

'LITTLE INDIANS'

While Colombian broadcasters were merely seen as entertaining curiosities, the riders they were there to cover fared much worse within the peloton.

Martín Ramírez, who won the 1984 Dauphiné Libéré, experienced what was perhaps the first in many unusual episodes that Colombian professionals continue to recount to this day. During the last stage of that race, Ramírez (who was wearing the leader's jersey but had only one team-mate left) was not welcomed warmly into the European peloton.

'I rode the entire stage on Hinault's wheel,' Ramírez remembered in British writer Matt Rendell's book *Kings of the Mountains*. 'He responded by braking hard to make me fall, while his team bombarded me with elbows and fists.'

Today, Ramírez believes that perhaps the European peloton was simply not used to change, and riders from a South American country beating them in major races – while still racing as amateurs – was simply too much for some to bear.

'No one knew who we were. Cochise [Rodríguez] had raced in Europe, but that had been long before. So it was clear that they saw us and called us "little Indians", "savages". We showed up all of a sudden, and managed to beat them in a big stage race on the eve of the Tour... Well, that just wasn't something they wanted. So the reception was not very good.'

Such was the treatment Colombians received that in 1984, while working for Colombia's RCN radio, French Olympic road champion José Beyaert nearly came to blows with Laurent Fignon over the matter.

Beyaert, a former boxer-turned-cyclist, had gone to Colombia in the early 1950s to race, and decided to stay. Now working as a radio commentator for a Colombian station, he overheard Fignon speaking about Colombian riders in a negative fashion and instantly felt the need to speak up. Matt Rendell, Beyaert's biographer, recounts, 'He [Beyaert] loved Colombia very, very deeply. It's for this reason that José threatened to break Laurent Fignon's jaw on one occasion at the finish line in the Tour de France, due to Fignon swearing about them.'

Though not driven to the brink of violence, Patrocinio Jiménez still has conflicting memories about those early Tours, including Fignon, who he remembers as 'unpleasant'. Asked why by the Colombian magazine *Cambio*, Jiménez points to Fignon's comment to a member of the press, in which he referred to Colombians as being from 'an inferior race'.

For the most part, however, the comments and reactions by both European riders and the press seemed to come about due to simple ignorance and lack of tact in regards to Colombia as a nation, as well as its people. For example, in the October 1985 issue of *Winning* magazine, an article by Noel Truyers titled, 'The Colombians Are Coming!', refers to the Café de Colombia team as an 'Indian cycling success'. Further showing his naïvety and ignorance, Truyers goes on to say that, at the time, electricity was 'still a city luxury' in Colombia, while television remained a 'show window rarity'. Neither was true, but both supported the misguided notion that Colombia was an uncivilised jungle – a view that is popular today.

Similarly, the French daily *Libération* ran an article on July 11, 1985, where Lucho Herrera's unwillingness to celebrate his victory at Saint-Étienne with champagne was said to be 'probably something that comes from his Indian culture'. So even as Colombian riders succeeded at the Tour, they continued to be treated a bit like a sideshow oddity.

While some may doubt the severity of the comments and treatment that Colombian riders received within the peloton, perhaps the clearest account of the matter comes from a seemingly unlikely source: American Andy Hampsten. While racing alongside Colombian riders, sometimes as a team-mate, Hampsten saw the treatment first hand.

'I saw how Colombians were treated unfairly by many of the ignorant people in European racing. It was hard for me as a foreigner to live and race in Europe, but I did not have the racist problems that my Colombian brothers experienced.'

In the end, however, Hampsten feels that the Colombians got the last laugh.

'I imagine Colombian riders suffered more abuse in the 80s when they started racing in Europe, and they were polite enough not to react like the assholes we North Americans did. They were also better with their results, and winning big stages in the major tours is a nice revenge.'

A FIXTURE AT THE TOUR DE FRANCE

On July 16, 1984, Luis Alberto Herrera became the first Colombian to win a stage at the Tour de France. He was also the first amateur and first Latin American to do so. The Colombian masses, transistor radios in hand, wept. So too did the commentators. With Herrera's victory, the negative whispers within the peloton suddenly began to die down. Colombia's diminutive climber had achieved the very revenge that Hampsten speaks of. He had won a stage at the Tour de France, and so too would Fabio Parra, Nelson Rodríguez, Oliverio Rincón, Mauricio Soler, Chepe González, Félix Cárdenas and Santiago Botero in the coming years.

During the 1980s, Colombian riders (climbers in particular) became fixtures at the Tour. In 1986, the Tour had two Colombian teams (Café de Colombia and Postobón), while Fabio Parra managed a podium spot in 1988. Through this success, the number of Colombian professionals who chose to ride for foreign teams was relatively small, which in part explains the popularity of Lucho Herrera (who always rode for Colombian teams), versus Fabio Parra (who made the move to Spanish squad Kelme early on).

And while Café de Colombia and Postobón both took on foreign riders from time to time, largely to help their climbers make it through flat and windy stages of races like the Tour, the squads remained a mostly Colombian affair, even as the sport became more international.

BROUGHT TO TEARS

As the 1980s came to a close, and a new decade began, Colombian cycling at the Tour de France waned. Café de Colombia, easily the strongest symbol of South American cycling at the Tour, ended in 1990. The sponsorship stopped as coffee prices dropped by 60 per cent after the end of the International Coffee Pact.[3]

This meant many Colombian riders began to disperse among international teams. Café de Colombia's beloved Lucho Herrera made the switch to Postobón, along with his loyal *gregario*, Henry Cárdenas, who had been there to assist Herrera as he won the Vuelta a España three years earlier. But Postobón's days in Europe were numbered as well, despite the fact that Herrera managed to win the Dauphiné Libéré for the team in 1991.

The dream of an all-Colombian team leading one of its riders to victory at the Tour de France came to a close in a most inauspicious manner at the 1992 Tour. Throughout the race, Postobón's riders retired for different reasons, leaving director Raúl Mesa with a two-man squad as the peloton rode onto the Champs-Élysées. Making matters worse was the fact that one of the two finishers, Arunas Cepele, wasn't even Colombian. It was a crushing blow for Mesa, who burst into tears as the team car made its way through Paris.

Others noticed the Colombian team's disastrous Tour, including race organisers, which meant the end of Postobón's invites to European races.

With that, the team retreated to Colombia, where they continued to race with some success until 1995. But regardless of the team's victories in their home country, the era of Colombian teams at the Tour came to a close.

THE PLAGUES

To be fair to the Postobón team, however, it wasn't just their 1992 Tour performance that put an end to Colombia's chances in the sport's biggest race. In reality, the end of Colombian teams at the Tour came about due to a combination of forces, which one humorous bike shop owner in Bogotá once explained to me as 'the plagues'.

Although the term was used for comedic effect, there's actually some truth to it. That's because aside from the price of coffee dropping significantly in 1990, the nation's plantations were also overcome with an infestation of African coffee berry borer beetles.[4] Though their invasion of Colombia's countryside wasn't quite up to biblical standards, the tiny beetles still managed to destroy a high percentage of the nation's coffee plantations, taking with them a sizable chunk of the country's economy.

That a beetle had contributed to the end of Colombia's *escarabajos* is a painful coincidence that is not lost on at least one Colombian cycling fan.

Another contributing factor was a cultural shift away from cycling and towards football within Colombia. With the national team qualifying for the 1990 World Cup for the first time since 1962, the nation turned its attention to the team of underdogs that captured their imagination, much in the way that early Colombian cycling teams at the Tour had.

Corporate sponsors, like Postobón, were also entranced by the lure of football, and they chose to shift their sponsorship budgets accordingly.

Hector Urrego, who still works with RCN radio, found himself in the middle of that cultural shift.

'The press turned its attention to football, which was understandable. In an instant, the country became football-ised, if I can use such a made-up term. That's what it felt like, and it continued into the 1994 World Cup where Colombia qualified once again. That, coupled with the fact that Colombia's best riders were then forced to ride for foreign teams, largely as climbing *domestiques*, really brought things to a close. Had you gathered the best Colombian riders of the 90s or any time after in one Colombian team, you would see that things were not different in terms of talent. But the focus on one Colombian team wasn't there anymore.'

SICK AND TIRED OF BEING HUMILIATED

While it's obvious that several factors played a role in the end of teams like Café de Colombia and Postobón, at least one rider who spent time in both teams thinks another aspect of cycling's culture contributed as well.

Henry Cárdenas was one of Lucho Herrera's most trusted lieutenants. Cárdenas contributed greatly to Herrera's Vuelta a España victory in 1987, while also taking a stage (and nearly nabbing the overall) at the Dauphiné Libéré the same year. Asked about that period, particularly the end of Colombian teams, Cárdenas doesn't hesitate to answer.

In particular he feels that Colombian riders, who excelled at climbing, were the first to suffer as a result of many riders, sprinters included, suddenly being able to out-climb them.

'There was an obvious change in the early 90s.

When you train, you have ways of measuring your performance: best times and records on climbs. So you know how you're doing. I was training, doing well, but I would go to Europe and everyone would be so much faster all of a sudden.

'They were using something strong, something serious. It started with just a few riders, but then it seemed like everyone, just everyone, could beat us. They could all climb faster.'

This shift prompted Cárdenas to leave Europe. But it also had an effect on Colombian fans, who were set on seeing their heroes conquer every mountain pass at the Tour, while not understanding the seismic shifts that were occurring within the sport.

'In 1992 I was greatly disheartened by racing in Europe,' explains Cárdenas. 'I was sick and tired of being humiliated by cyclists who were doped up to their eyeballs with EPO, while I had no opportunities of winning anything while racing clean. But even more maddening was the way I was criticised by the press, at least certain Colombian journalists, who were not capable of understanding the fundamental change that was happening in cycling. I'm speaking of the new types of doping that became popular in the 1990s. They didn't have the guts to explain to Colombian fans why our riders could no longer ride and compete like in the days of Lucho and Fabio Parra. They accused us of being lazy and of having become bourgeois over time. It was incredibly unfair.'

...THE MORE THINGS STAY THE SAME

Despite the end of Postobón and Café de Colombia, and the rise in football's popularity, the country's love affair with cycling never died. Colombia, a nation that has endured hardship in every imaginable sense for its entire history, simply seems to understand the martyrdom that is inherent in cycling.

So too does it collectively enjoy its beauty. The sport remains seamlessly woven into the country's cultural fabric, with countless cycling academies, teams and races playing a major role in developing young riders into top-level talent. Proof of this is the quality and quantity of Colombian riders competing at the highest levels of the sport today, along with Team Colombia, a state-sponsored squad hoping for a Tour de France invitation within the next two years. In fact, the sheer number of Colombian riders in Europe today, along with the promising potential they hold, could possibly manage to surpass the accomplishments of past generations, including the glory years of the 1980s. Such is the enduring passion for cycling that remains in Colombia.

Looking around Colombia's cycling landscape today, from youth academies, to development teams, it becomes obvious that regardless of whether a Colombian entity or corporation chooses to sponsor a team or not, cycling will always be part of the nation's collective consciousness.

It's part of Colombian life. It's not a sport, a hobby or a pastime. It's part of Colombia itself. And that, perhaps, is the very illness that Gabriel García Márquez wrote about in 1955 as he saw countless Colombians ride their bikes maniacally through Bogotá's streets. It's an illness that will always drive Colombians to get on their bikes and start pedalling, and given the country's topography, that will always mean going steeply uphill.

SOURCES
[1 2 3 4] Rendell, Matt. *Kings of the Mountains*, Aurum Press 2002

Klaus Bellon Gaitán was born and raised in Bogotá, Colombia. In the summer of 1984, he woke before dawn to listen to Tour de France on the radio. Today, he lives in the United States with his wife, and their miniature dachshund Emma and still wakes up early to watch and listen to the Tour in July. He has written about architecture, music and design, co-authoring *Typography for the People: Hand-Painted Signs from Around the World* with his brother Daniel. He writes a blog, www.cyclinginquisition.com and has contributed to *Road*, *Peloton* and *Cycle Sport* magazines. He keeps his toothbrush in a Café de Colombia mug with Patronicio Jiménez's face on. When Klaus mentioned this during their interview, Jiménez did not seem particularly impressed or flattered.

5

For journalists covering the Tour, the hire car is not just a mode of transport. It becomes a mobile office and transport café.

Brendan Gallagher describes what it's like trying to keep up with the world's greatest sporting spectacle when it keeps pedalling away from him.

There's a lot more to it than following the sat-nav and singing along to The Bee Gees on the stereo...

IT'S ALL ABOUT THE CAR

BY BRENDAN GALLAGHER

It's not about the bike – it's all about the car. The Tour de France is many things but for working journalists it is primarily a white-knuckled rally around France and neighbouring countries chasing deadlines and stories, searching for wifi hotspots and petrol stations on remote mountainsides at midnight and praying that your hotel, booked absent-mindedly on the internet six months earlier, actually exists.

Stress and excitement mix in equal measure and, if the latter carries you all the way to Paris, it is, thankfully, the latter that stays with you forever.

In the quiet depths of winter, as you lie sleepless in the coal-black dark, it is the vivid light and mind-consuming noise of that rally that looms largest as Tour thoughts randomly present themselves for processing and evaluation.

Your mind hurtles around a country boasting more varied landscapes than most continents. There is just too much going on at the time to do anything other than passively observe and absorb. The epic stages and finishes are great – of course they are –

and the riders endlessly fascinating, but you get to write about them every day. You cover the Tour to the best of your ability, freeze the frame of the big days in your mind, decide your version of the story whether you be right or wrong, and move on. In cycling terms, yesterday becomes instant history; last night might as well be last year.

As a result, it is everything else that constantly assaults your mind and 'everything else' essentially involves life in a car, with your travelling companions, moving from stage start to stage finish and then onto a new hotel every day for 21 days.

That is your world and frankly how can it be otherwise when you spend up to ten hours a day, more often than not with two or three fellow human beings who might well be friends but are also professional rivals, in a space no bigger than a decent-sized kitchen table?

During the course of that month – from the moment you abandon your loved ones and wave goodbye to any semblance of normality – your car becomes your universe. Not only is it your means of transport, with every change of engine noise and unaccounted-for flashing light causing consternation and palpitations, but it is your office, place of refuge and, occasionally, even your bedroom.

It is the talking shop where the events of the day and yesteryear are minutely dissected and knowing verdicts arrived at; it is a canteen in which the ubiquitous baguette and takeaway pasta dishes are consumed on an industrial scale around the clock and it is the library where *L'Equipe* is religiously read every morning along with the ASO Tour route book or bible, as it is known. Although we tend to swear at rather than on it.

Recorded interviews are laboriously transcribed on the hoof – 'Bloody hell! Did he really say that? Good line. Complete and utter lies, mind' – and music is played both to soothe and to energise, or sometimes even to deliberately accompany the glorious vistas that only the Tour can provide.

Wagner or The Smiths for a brooding rainy day in the Alps, Strauss or perhaps The Eagles for the sunny Pyrenees, Bachman-Turner Overdrive or U2 for a blast down the motorway, a bit of Rod Stewart, Adele or Miles Davis for those more mellow, late-evening drives.

I've occasionally got away with my Bollywood Greatest Hits and a much treasured Best of Brazilian CD, but The Bee Gees are summarily rejected by my travelling companions. Philistines. One colleague compiled a deliberately upbeat CD full of sing-along numbers and disco classics that we always saved for Saturday morning just to lift our spirits at the start of yet another busy weekend. For some reason – no matter how tired, knackered and grumpy – *Happy Hour* by The Housemartins will always put a smile back on my face and restore good humour.

Sat-nav becomes something of a hate figure on most Tours and is verbally abused on an almost daily basis. Mobile phones are lost or mislaid hourly and your mood – I much prefer cycling's use of the word 'morale', which confers dignity and gravity to some pretty appalling sulks and outbursts – changes by the minute. Life and your car become indivisible. You can't remember one without the other.

It all starts so serenely. In recent years I have collected my chariot of choice – I am delighted to shamelessly give Skoda UK a plug at this juncture in the sure knowledge that the esteemed editors of this book have also benefited from their largesse – and head for Folkestone and the Eurotunnel with scarcely a backwards glance.

Tour fever is already beginning to grip, but as you disappear under *la Manche* there first follows the strangest prelude to the madness. Half an hour of completely nothing. You snooze in the car *sans* radio or companions, who await your arrival at the *Grand Départ* venue, and, being British, you just can't be bothered to climb out and talk to your fellow travellers. The carriage rocks and creaks gently, a bizarrely nautical sensation 300 feet below the sea, and your mind ticks over gently in neutral or conjures up the screech of seagulls and the whiff of seaweed. Truly the calm before the storm.

The car? You need a GC model. To drive and finish the Tour de France you need something with a big engine, proven reliability and the endurance of a Brad Wiggins that is going to eat up the 6,000 kilometres or so that await.

Above all else, you need comfort, so curb your boy-racer tendencies and opt for an estate so you can dump your bags out of sight and maximise the living space elsewhere. A top tip, though: don't even think about roof racks. Completely hopeless. You will lose everything many times over as you career around thousands of bends. Just don't go there.

The ideal number of passengers? Let me save you more time and much heartache here. The answer, despite what the psychologists will tell you, is unequivocally three.

Driving the entire Tour on your own is just too stressful to offer any real enjoyment, unless you are a compulsive loner and have no issues with chronic sleep deprivation. Two, more often than not, is a complete nightmare with 'the happy couple' invariably falling out.

I've been lucky, but I've witnessed so many acrimonious divorces on the Tour that I couldn't possibly recommend it with a clear conscience. The glory of three is that it provides the much-needed safety valve of always having somebody to bitch with about the other guy!

These things are important. Four is way too crowded, by the way, and also leads to cabals, factions and arguments.

Three also works logistically. One to drive, one to organise the sat-nav and music in the front, and one to snooze in the back or tap away on their latest piece – which always starts out as an award-winning story or definitive insight but somehow gets dragged raggedly along by the Tour's ever-turning wheels.

At this stage, it is probably also worth mentioning the subtle game of musical chairs that evolves as to who sits where and when.

Firstly, always be mindful that if you intend to drive the route on a big mountain day the only seat worth having is the driver's so that you can strap in properly and anticipate every hairpin and bend. Everywhere else in the car resembles a huge laundrette-style tumble dryer. Driving the car on such days is probably the most fun you can legally have outside of an RAC Rally and… well, perhaps we'd better not go there.

Beware, too, the long, lazy transfer, perhaps involving some motorways, and grabbing that inviting front passenger seat where you can stretch your legs, control the sounds and soak up the sun as you dangle your left arm luxuriantly out of the window. The massive downside is that in an English left-hand-drive car you will also be the man required to pay at every *péage* on the motorways, and when the final day of financial reckoning comes in Paris, you will almost certainly have lost your receipts and will be miserably out of pocket.

In the front passenger seat you will also be held responsible for map-reading duties when the sat-nav goes moody, and will have to spend most of the day answering the driver's mobile phone. In fact, you will often be reduced to a mere *domestique*, so be warned.

Finally, just be alert if your previously supine mate suddenly absolutely insists on doing all the driving one quiet day after a week of complete sloth on his part: 'No, really, I want to, my pleasure, you've done all the graft so far.' You can be almost certain that it will be because he requires a big favour the next day.

If you really do need a favour – perhaps you've got a day on one of the Tour motorbikes organised and need to go AWOL, or have lined up that elusive 'exclusive' interview you have been chasing for months – then make yourself popular and clean the car out one night.

Rotting bananas, crushed empty water-bottles, sweaty cheeses, stale baguettes, chewing gum, discarded T-shirts, and the rest of the Tour's debris. This is not a job for the faint-hearted, but earns you millions of brownie points that can be cashed-in to your huge advantage.

The Tour, for me, officially starts when a drop-dead gorgeous French PR lady relents and presents you with the green car stickers without which nothing is remotely possible on the Tour de France.

With the stickers proudly displayed front and

rear, and your press accreditation dangling around your neck with the swagger of Medallion Man, you are king of all you survey.

Short of winning an Olympic gold medal or the lottery, I can't imagine anything finer. You can drive and park anywhere, habitually get saluted at by French police on the race route and join high speed evacuations down a mountain after a summit finish. You even get people wandering over to your car and asking you for an autograph in case you are some-body famous.

Unsurprisingly, these stickers are gold dust and I am indebted to American freelance Gregor Brown – a hardened veteran of the road – for the most cunning of tips a few years back after I had a rear sticker stolen overnight.

What you do is this. Smooth the stickers out on the window corners, as ordered by race organisers ASO, and then reach into your pocket for your car keys. Then make diagonal scores with the sharp end of your key across both stickers – six or seven will be enough – and stand back and admire your work. Now if somebody tries to 'lift' them, they will come off in six or seven severed sections and will be com-pletely unusable. Genius. The 'scoring out' ceremony is now an entrenched part of my annual Tour de France ritual, giving me a ridiculous amount of smug satisfaction.

It can, in all honesty, be hell on four wheels

out there. I have no words to describe the abject misery of being stuck in a monster four-hour traffic jam in temperatures in excess of a hundred degrees when the air-con fails.

Every Tour has at least one – and sometimes two or three stamina-sapping traffic jams – and my memory is that they tend to be on Friday nights or Sunday evenings. Frustratingly, such jams tend to inch forward and never come to a complete halt, so although I am no fan of automatic cars, I make an exception for the Tour when they really come into their own and prevent RSI of the left ankle.

The most torturous day in my Tour history was being stuck in such a jam in 2007 at the end of the Col d'Aubisque stage when Wiggins' then team-mate Cristian Moreni had been arrested at the finish, and Wiggins and his Cofidis team had been escorted down the mountain by the police.

It was a huge story by any criteria, especially for the British press. The good news was that I got Brad on his mobile on the team bus straight away to get the full details of what was happening. The bad news was that 30 seconds later we lost all mobile signals for the next three hours as we disappeared into the black hole of a Tour traffic jam. I still wake up in a cold sweat.

Shoes, strangely, are a recurring theme on Tour de France road trips – mainly because of the constant and unsavoury desire to take them off once you reach the safety of the car and settle in for a long drive. Twice I have left a pair of shoes in William Fotheringham's Tour wagon. He generously posted one pair back to me on our return to 'Blighty' but had another pair destroyed on public-hygiene grounds.

Shoes also played their part in a curious episode involving a colleague who, for professional reasons, should probably remain nameless. For the time being anyway. Journalist X and his companions were two weary hours into a sweaty drive to Bordeaux when he realised he had left a rather natty pair of patent-leather Spanish shoes in his previous hotel room that his girlfriend – soon to be his fiancée and ultimately his wife – had bought for him. Ah, there's nice.

Panic-stricken, he immediately demanded the car to be turned around from whence it came, raced two long hours back to the hotel and then set sail again for Bordeaux on a chaotic Friday evening where his fuming party arrived 20 minutes after a dramatic stage win for Cav. A pair of shoes or your career? It seems a no-brainer, but the Tour de France inspires a fine kind of madness, and you can lose the plot at any moment.

That's one reason I always lend a sympathetic ear to riders who explode in fits of rage or display odd character traits. When Mark Renshaw head-butted a path through for Cavendish at the finish at Bourg-lès-Valence in 2011, was I alone in quietly cheering 'The Bathurst Brawler' on? I have done the same many times, metaphorically speaking, on the Tour. Let he who is without sin cast the first stone.

When I write 'cheering' Renshaw along at Bourg-lès-Valence, I am being rather economical with the truth. I was actually in front of a television in a blissfully cool bar in Die about an hour away after yet another hellish day that had started with a two-hour drive to the stage start in Sisteron because a colleague, Journalist Y, had arranged to spend the day on one of the official Tour motorbikes – one of the hottest tickets in world sport.

We dropped him off, then retraced our steps only to hit a traffic jam and then, somewhere on the road outside of Gap, we suffered a rare double blow-out of our offside wheels.

It was 108 degrees in the shade – siesta time, and so nobody was around. We only had one spare wheel and, for a couple of hours as we festered roadside, I seriously considered quitting journalism.

Eventually we got it sorted and drove like the wind to try to get to the finish of the stage. We soon realised it was going to be impossible, so we pulled into Die and sought refuge in a bar with the TV on. All this time, the misery was compounded by the fact that our hotel the previous evening was less than an hour's drive from the finish at Bourg-lès-Valence. The easiest day of the Tour on paper. It was, shall we say, a tad frosty at the dinner table that night when our happy band of travellers were all finally reunited.

But the good moments and friendship are worth every second. No, seriously. A blissful, breezy sunny day cruising ahead of the peloton in Provence, stopping only to stock up on ripe peaches and cherries, or a crisp morning in the high mountains about an hour ahead of the race with the roads closed, seemingly just for you, make it all worth it.

The contrasts on the big climbs can be extraordinary. On one side of the mountain the best part of half a million people are roadside creating their own riot of noise and colour. And just over the top of the summit line, less than 30 seconds by car down the descent, the sheep are wandering over the road and it's so peaceful you can hear the bees buzzing as you pull over for a call of nature.

The descents are very special, and for me provide the greatest spectacle of the Tour. They are also the biggest challenge, driving-wise, if you are in a hurry: a top cyclist can descend much quicker than any car or motorcyclist.

There are also moments of private satisfaction on the road when miraculously you make just the right call. Just. After the final time trial finished at Pauillac in 2010, we faced the certainty of a grinding, three-hour traffic jam just to get back into Bordeaux before heading north to Paris.

Or we could taken a huge punt and head north up the D1215 to the end of the peninsular where rumour had it a special ferry might or might not be running from Le Verdon-sur-Mer to Royan.

The fearsome tourist-board lady insisted there was no Saturday-evening ferry, and flourished the ferry timetable by way of confirmation. But the locals in our adopted café defiantly said, '*Oui, oui* – be there by 7.30pm.'

My frazzled colleagues, perhaps wearying of our non-stop race against the clock around France, were reluctant, but I suddenly came over all authoritative and defiant. The chase was on – more Keystone Kops than Steve McQueen – but glory be there, 40 minutes later, bobbing away in a tiny harbour, was a comically small car ferry just getting up steam.

We slammed on the brakes outside a tin shack, euros were thrown in the general direction of a ticket officer who was clearly just packing up for the day, and the deal was done. High fives all round.

Never has a cold Coke tasted better as we crossed the Gironde estuary on a gorgeous summer's evening having effectively bought ourselves four or five hours in the long run up to Paris. We even had time to stop at a little fish restaurant on the other side: our only sit-down dinner of the entire trip. Ah, *la belle France*.

Everybody should experience at least one high-speed mountain evacuation before they shuffle of this mortal coil. In fact, I'm thinking of marketing them as an extreme sport.

There are two kinds. The first are the strictly

organised official expeditions, which are nonetheless transmitted exclusively by word of mouth around the huge press room during the day.

There is no advertisement as such – otherwise the public would want to join in. When in doubt, I just ask a driver from the agency AFP or *L'Equipe*. Yes, the big French media operations have their own dedicated drivers.

Anyway, we meet at the ski-lift car park at 8pm – it's always the ski-lift car park – and the white-gloved police motorbike riders assemble in formation at the front of our peloton with lights flashing and horns blaring. These are the heroes who will guide you down the wrong side of the road to the bottom of the valley some 25 kilometres distant, thus doing away with the need to queue.

Strangely, even the most committed socialist members of the press corps have no problem with this flagrant elitism.

But these hurtling plunges into the unknown come with a health warning. In fact, don't even think of enlisting unless you are prepared to drive at the same speed as the highly trained outriders.

This is a runaway train that bears comparison with the HTC-Highroad team of old, and stops for nothing. If you lose the wheel of the car in front, the whole thing fractures, the train is derailed, and you get two or three hundred of the world's media cursing you. No pressure, then.

Alas, official evacuations are few and far between and it's the unofficial, ad-hoc evacuations that I have grown to love, and indeed flatter myself to be something of an expert on.

These happen when the jersey winners, or those required for doping control, come down the mountain in a team car rather later than the team buses and are accompanied by a single police motorcyclist.

And this can be really tricky. You need to spot the single flashing blue light out of your mirror, a long way back, jump on their tail the instant they pass, and then hang on for dear life like some vagrant train-hopper from a 1920s movie.

Gradually, everybody else does the same, and soon an unofficial rogue train builds and morphs into an official evacuation. As long as you possess the sacred green sticker, the police en route and at the valley bottom still tend to turn a blind eye to your gross impertinence.

The joy of arriving at the bottom of the valley or your motorway junction three hours ahead of schedule is only matched, I should add, by the relief of living to fight another day.

Actually, there is a third form of mountain evacuation. Remember earlier when I motioned that the Tour can drive anybody mad at any time?

Well, in recent years I have 'driven the Tour' with Matt McGeehan of the Press Association – as steady a driver and Tour 'oppo' as you could hope to encounter, and very much an upright citizen. But then one night, after our travel people had idiotically booked us into Les Deux Alpes instead of Alpe d'Huez – three miles away as the crow flies, but a five-hour drive up and down the valley in bad traffic after a stage – he lost it in spectacular fashion.

This was a crack of Miguel Indurain proportions. We had covered about 400 metres in the previous hour, waiting in vain for one of my 'type two' evacuations, when Matt just suddenly yanked our car into the wrong lane, started honking the horn, and embarked on his own virtuoso display of descending worthy of Fabian Cancellara or Vincenzo Nibali in their prime. *Chapeau*!

Just as the slightly eerie Eurotunnel experience marks the start of the Tour, there comes a moment when you know the rally around France is drawing to a close. All too often it is just a weary arrival back at Calais in the middle of the night, dog-tired as the fatigue starts hitting you in waves, but one year it was an altogether more classy affair.

It was about 7.30am on the final Sunday morning, and we had already been up and driving for an hour or more on the motorway heading to the Champs-Élysées some 350 kilometres ahead of us. Our speed – and let's err on the side of caution here – was gently nudging 160 kilometres per hour as we hogged the empty middle lane.

But then, in the rearview mirror, was a sight to

turn the blood cold. Four pelotons of 12 French police motorcyclists, ramrod straight, riding three abreast in prefect formation, down the fast lane at fully 200 kilometres per hour.

As the lead peloton drew level and I grappled with possible excuses for our excess speed, the officer with the most stripes looked over, smiled as he clocked the green stickers, and then saluted smartly before going on his untroubled way.

Although grossly unequal in the eyes of the law – he was the law for God's sake – there was a tacit acknowledgement that we had all been on the same extraordinary journey over the last month, and that now was not the time to quibble over something so petty as a speeding fine. *Vive le Tour!*

Brendan Gallagher has been a sports journalist for 30 years, serving his apprenticeship in South Wales and as a director of Hayters Sports Agency before a 20-year stint at the coalface with the *Daily Telegraph*, proudly writing on any sport except football. He has ghosted Irish rugby union player Brian O'Driscoll's autobiography as well as *In Pursuit of Glory* and *On Tour* for Brad Wiggins. He also wrote the official LOCOG history of Great Britain and the Olympics ahead of the 2012 Games. In a lighter vein, he indulged his love of comic-book heroes by compiling biographical histories of Wilson of the Wizard, Alf Tupper – the Tough of the Track – and Roy of the Rovers in *Sporting Supermen*.

6

It wasn't long ago that Germany's Linus Gerdemann was being touted as The Next Jan Ullrich – albeit unafraid to talk about the fight against doping.

Just six summers after taking the Tour's yellow jersey at Le Grand Bornand, Gerdemann found himself without a contract.

Why, asks **Daniel Friebe**, is Gerdemann on the verge of disappearing from the sport having once looked like being one of its saviours?

THE RELUCTANT PRINCE

BY DANIEL FRIEBE

It was one of those July afternoons when the Tour de France seemed to exist for the sole purpose of making ordinary life's rich tapestry appear drab and monochrome.

The sun blazed. The Alps glistened. Every scene was saturated with colour and, as the race drew near, noise. The French, celebrating their national holiday, Bastille Day, at the umpteenth *Tour du Renouveau*, or 'Tour of Renewal', still cheering and raising their tumblers of rosé because, well, *'Le Tour, c'est le Tour.'* In spite of everything. Dutch and Belgians were spilling out of their camping cars. A few bereft Americans. A smaller number of early-to-the-party Brits and Aussies.

They didn't all know or necessarily recognise Linus Gerdemann, but they would by the end of the day. Gerdemann had gone clear in a 15-man move early in this seventh stage of the 2007 Tour de France to Le Grand Bornand, and over the next 160 kilometres he would unfasten those breakaway companions from his wheel one by one.

Finally, with 20 kilometres to go, halfway up the Col de la Colombière, the Kazakh Dmitriy Fofonov was the last rider to see Gerdemann's magenta jersey disappearing into the heat haze. Half an hour later, a day short of ten years after compatriot Jan Ullrich at Andorra, Gerdemann was winning the first mountain-top stage of the Tour and taking the yellow jersey. The next morning, the German tabloid *Bild* quoted Ullrich's coach, Peter Becker: 'Linus has the same talent as Jan.'

Ullrich, of course, was one perverse reason why the day felt so special. A year earlier, Germany's one and only Tour de France winner had left the Tour in disgrace following revelations about his dangerous liaisons with Dr Eufemiano Fuentes. Kaiser Jan had been the catalyst for an overnight boom in cycling in his home country in the late 1990s, but, by cheating and getting caught in 2006, he had caused a sudden meltdown. It had emerged in the wake of Operación Puerto that systematic doping had gone on in the team that was now T-Mobile for years. Even Erik Zabel had dabbled. Bjarne Riis had done much more than that. The result, over a decade on, was that the team's destiny now lay in the hands of an American telecommunications magnate, Bob Stapleton, brought in to fight the fire, and in the legs of a new wave of purportedly clean riders like Gerdemann.

There were therefore clear parallels but also striking differences between Ullrich and Gerdemann, who happened to live in the same Swiss village on the shores of Lake Constance.

Many were apparent that evening in Le Grand Bornand, when Gerdemann arrived in his post-race press conference, his golden mane swept back under a T-Mobile baseball cap. More than once, he was asked about doping, and at each invitation he spoke willingly and, it seemed, sincerely.

'I just want to say thanks,' he said in fluent English, 'to all the people who still believe in the sport, at a time when it has big, big problems.'

On the challenge of restoring the sport's tattered credibility, he added, 'I think it's really hard for young riders to take all the responsibility, but the sport has given a lot to me, and I think now is the time to give something back.'

Beside the stage, T-Mobile's communications chief purred. It could easily have been a rehearsed speech. In fact, Gerdemann was ad-libbing.

You couldn't help being impressed – except when he got up off his chair and turned to leave. For all his well-documented weight problems, by the time Ullrich got to the Tour every year, he radiated power and athleticism from every sculpted muscle and pro-truding vein; on the eve of every *Grand Départ*, he would sweep into the *Permanence*, the race HQ, for his pre-race press conference, escorted by a giddy entou-rage of T-Mobile staff, and the whole room would suppress a gasp. Gerdemann, by contrast, was more

likely to provoke frowns. If on the bike he was no
paragon of elegance, off it his stubby legs, long torso
and sloping shoulders didn't scream Tour winner
either. To be kind, you might have said Greg LeM-
ond. To be cruel, you couldn't help but think, 'face
of a Backstreet Boy, body of a Bash Street Kid'.

That, in hindsight, might have been the first
clue. No one, though, was in the mood for realism.
Except, that was, Gerdemann, who explained that
he had a long way to go and couldn't gauge yet his
potential as a grand tour rider. The German press
listened, perhaps agreed, but ladled on the hyperbole
regardless. The hook of Ullrich's ten-year anniversary was too inviting to ignore.

Andreas Buckert, who was covering that Tour
for the *Süddeutsche Zeitung*, remembers, 'It was quite a
special moment. It was the kind of story the German
audience was looking for, after the big mess the
previous year. He was fresh-faced, he seemed to be
convincing, and he was very happy to talk about anti-
doping when asked. Even when he lost the yellow
jersey the next day, the German public saw that as a
positive thing. Ah, you see, they said, that shows he's
clean. He can't recover. He could do no wrong.'

Gerdemann struggled into Tignes in 20th place
the next day, over five minutes behind a nearly
nuclear Michael Rasmussen. The yellow jersey
was gone, but events soon conspired to position
T-Mobile and Gerdemann at the centre of the

narrative once again. Gerdemann's team-mate, Patrik Sinkewitz, had collided with a spectator on his way to the team hotel and was out of the race. So was Michael Rogers after his crash on the descent of the Cormet de Roselend. Worse – much worse – news followed a few hours later: Sinkewitz had tested positive for synthetic testosterone. It was the last straw for German TV networks ARD and ZDF, who packed up and went home.

Deprived of the exposure that the biggest budget in professional cycling was supposed to buy, it seemed certain that T-Mobile would also soon be following through on threats to pull the plug. The team itself decided to stay in France only after a crisis meeting back at their team hotel and a stirring call to arms from their most experienced rider, Axel Merckx. Gerdemann told the press that he had no sympathy for Sinkewitz, no understanding whatsoever for how someone could put his team-mates' livelihoods in danger. When he called Sinkewitz in hospital, it was a short, dutiful enquiry about his injuries. Doping wasn't mentioned.

Linus Gerdemann went on to finish the 2007 Tour de France in 35th position. It was a respectable performance for a 24-year-old riding his second three-week race (he had finished 72nd in the 2005 Vuelta with CSC), particularly in a race so ravaged by doping scandals that Gerdemann's use of the present tense – 'cycling has big problems', not 'cycling had big

problems' – seemed perfectly justified. Who knew
how far he could go if those issues were resolved?
To the very top – the top of the Tour? Some believed
so. Gerdemann's old CSC boss, Bjarne Riis, opined
that, 'Linus can achieve whatever he wants. It's just
up to him to decide where he wants to go.'

* * *

Six years have passed. Six years. Incredible to think
that's all it is. Not because it doesn't seem a long time –
it definitely does – but because it's still a long journey
from the gates of paradise to the bowels of oblivion,
even in the fickle world of professional sport. Others
have fallen from grace faster, but they have taken
familiar shortcuts: ill-discipline, booze, drugs of the
recreational or performance-enhancing kind, women.
Or, more mundanely, injuries and illness. But Linus
Gerdemann can point the finger at none of these
things. His has been less fall than fizzle. Not a lesson
in self-sabotage, the titillating story of a prodigy who
achieved and was promised too much, too soon, but
the infinitely more mysterious and anticlimactic tale
of a young man who never quite found his path,
or his place. Probably not, after all, the 'cautionary
tale of squandered talent and blinding self-interest'
described by his former manager Bob Stapleton, but
something more complex and poignant.

This July, barring a miracle, Linus Gerdemann

won't be at the Tour de France, except perhaps as a spectator when the race arrives on the Côte d'Azur, near his Monaco home, on the fourth day. In June, where usually he'd have been tapering towards optimum condition, he'll most likely be spending time at his other property in Deià, Majorca, with his girlfriend, an English-born, Monaco-based model and TV presenter named Louise Prieto. Gerdemann will be riding his bike for two or three hours a day, still hoping he hasn't pinned his last *dossard* to his back, but at the same time he'll know that with every passing week or month his prospects of returning to the pro peloton become a little more bleak.

A year ago, if you had told him that he'd soon be out of a job, he would have thought you were joking. In 2011, he had won the Tour of Luxembourg, delighting Leopard-Trek's notoriously cantankerous owner Flavio Becca. The following summer, he claims now, he had assurances from the team's top brass that his contract would be renewed. But, says Leopard-Trek general manager Luca Guercilena, 'It may be that the previous management and Johan Bruyneel told him that he would stay.'

The reality once Bruyneel was sent on his way and Guercilena took control in October, says the Italian, was that, 'We came quite close to an agreement but Linus's manager was just asking a bit too much.'

The manager and his client then separated, amicably, in December, shortly before the procycling circus rolled out of town for the 2013 season without Gerdemann.

Some, and not only Gerdemann, were baffled. Rolf Aldag, his former *directeur sportif* at T-Mobile, says now, 'It's very, very strange. It's just not logical that a guy who took the yellow jersey at the Tour, and who only 18 months ago won the Tour of Luxembourg, should be unemployed. He's not suspicious – and that's so important now. You have to be sure of the riders you sign, and you can be of Linus. I have no idea why he wouldn't get a deal.'

There are also those who don't share Aldag's surprise. Gerdemann and Jörg Jaksche were never team-mates, and Jaksche's involvement in Operación Puerto seemed to place them on opposite sides of the moral divide. Nonetheless, now reinvented as a vocal anti-doping advocate, Jaksche says that he has seen enough of Gerdemann to believe that his current predicament is at partly self-inflicted.

'Am I really surprised? Not really,' Jaksche says. 'In cycling, when you're in a position like the one Linus was in last year, often it's your friends who save you. A good example is the way Andreas Klöden helped Danilo Hondo to get a deal with RadioShack this year. Now, I never had the feeling that Linus had many friends. He always came across as a bit superior, a bit arrogant. People also thought he perhaps spoke a bit too much about anti-doping. Maybe that also explains why he's out of the sport now…'

Jaksche, it should be pointed out, comes to this debate with a vested interest. This, after all, is a man who used to sign his text messages: 'The best-looking German rider behind Linus Gerdemann.'

* * *

Gerdemann was an anomaly in professional cycling the day he arrived, dragging a Louis Vuitton suitcase across the hotel car park at his first Team CSC training camp. Almost from that moment, he came with another kind of baggage, whose connotations seemed to cause him discomfort.

'I come from a normal, middle-class household; I wasn't born with a silver spoon in my mouth,' he protested in one interview with German magazine *Tour*. That may have been true, but there still weren't many sons of psychiatrists in the professional peloton. The other German wunderkind tipped for Tour de France glory, Markus Fothen, was the child of pig-farmers.

Born and raised in Münster, an elegant university town voted the world's most liveable city in 2004, Gerdemann started racing bikes relatively late.

Aged 15, he fell off a shopping bike, broke his shin, and a doctor prescribed... more cycling, as part of his rehabilitation. Soon he had borrowed a friend's road bike and was entering competitions. In his first full season, he won eight times.

The victories flowed over the next six summers, as did the plaudits. Riding for the Winfix team, he won the season-long German under-23 Bundesliga in both 2003 and 2004 – but, puzzlingly, was never selected for the German world championship squad in that category. The national coach, Peter Weibel, said that candidates for selection were mandatorily required to race in certain events, and that Gerdemann and his team had refused. Winfix replied that it was a silly rule. They also suggested that the German Federation had hindered Gerdemann's hunt for a pro contract by portraying him as a 'troublemaker'. The label, and Weibel's assertion that Gerdemann was 'not a team player', proved hard to dispel.

Even back then, Gerdemann was dividing opinion. For every Weibel, there was a Marcel Wüst, the retired German sprinter, who worked as Winfix's press officer in the two years that Gerdemann spent at the third division team. Wüst remembers a mature, ambitious young man armed with a steely resolve. The week before the under-23 German road race championship in 2004, Gerdemann collapsed, exhausted, into a chair on Wüst's terrace, wasted by the latest in a series of punishing training sessions.

'He was doing this extreme carbo-load, and it was quite impressive to see how committed he was,' Wüst remembers. 'Most kids at that age are all over the place when they attempt something like that. Then of course Linus went and won the race. I used to love him, as the team's press guy,' Wüst goes on, 'because he would say interesting things and say them well. He was the first rider I'd call to do stuff.'

Brian Nygaard, the Team CSC communications chief, felt exactly the same when Gerdemann finally scored a pro deal with that team the following year.

'He was well-spoken, clean-cut. I thought, "Yeah, we can do something with this kid,"' Nygaard says.

Recommended to Riis by Jens Voigt, Gerdemann impressed at a pre-season training camp in Tuscany with his riding as much as with his designer luggage. His first race for the team was the Four Days of Dunkirk, where he wore the leader's jersey for one day and wound up fifth overall. His second was the Bayern Rundfahrt, where he finished third on general classification, and his third was the Tour of Switzerland. There, Riis's claim that Linus Gerdemann was 'the next Jan Ullrich' suddenly began to make sense. Eight kilometres from the finish of a lumpy stage seven into Lenk, Gerdemann sequestered himself into last position of a six-man breakaway group, waited for his moment, then pounced mercilessly. He was 22 and a stage winner in one of the world's biggest races. The kid patently had class.

Having overlooked him once, T-Mobile now realised that the biggest German team could hardly afford not to have the biggest German talent in its number. Olaf Ludwig, T-Mobile's then-manager, made Gerdemann an offer for the 2007 season, and Gerdemann went back to Riis to see whether he would match it. Riis said no, and added that he wasn't in the business of developing riders so that they could then be cherry-picked by rival teams. He could leave now, a year early, Riis told Gerdemann.

'He wanted too much, and he hasn't shown enough yet. He went for the money – that's his right. I'm not angry with him,' Riis assured the press. He was more aggrieved with T-Mobile for 'tapping up' a rider they had ignored a few months earlier.

T-Mobile didn't care – they were thrilled. In T-Mobile colours, Gerdemann won nothing in 2006, but his progress continued. Top tens on the general classification in the Volta a Catalunya and the Tour of Switzerland augured well for T-Mobile's succession plan – Ullrich eventually handing over to Gerdemann. Eventually, or, as it turned out, immediately. The Tour of Switzerland, which Ullrich won in large part thanks to Gerdemann's Trojan efforts in the mountains, turned out to be the older man's last race for T-Mobile, and the last race of his career.

Two weeks later, on the eve of the Tour, Ullrich or *Hijo de Rudicio* – 'Son of Rudy', referring to T-Mobile *directeur sportif* Rudy Pevenage – as Eufemiano Fuentes liked to call him, was swallowed up by Operación Puerto.

Germany would wait a year, only a year, until that technicolour July 2007 afternoon, for Gerdemann to show that he was a worthy heir. Or so they thought.

* * *

'Linus was never going to be another Ullrich.'

Rolf Aldag, part of the new T-Mobile management regime charged with reinventing the team in the second half of the 2006 season, tells it like it is and like it always was. No one is more surprised than Aldag that Gerdemann finds himself unemployed and staring at the end of his career at age 30, but, at the same time, Aldag says, it should have been clear to everyone even in 2007 that the comparisons with Ullrich were vastly overblown.

'We knew he had talent, and we didn't now where it would lead. But we saw Linus's limitations pretty much straight away over the couple of days after he took the jersey,' Aldag points out. 'He had good power, which put him in a position to win races, but he was quite a long way from being able to challenge in major tours.'

That naked reality, though, was lost in a maelstrom of hype. Seduced by Gerdemann's frequent and convincing pronouncements on doping, the media cast him, if not as 'the next Ullrich', then at least as 'the future', without always specifying what that meant. If it referred to the message that he continually sent out in interviews about how the sport couldn't continue in its present vein of self-harm then, yes, it was somewhat justified.

If, however, they were confusing spin and

rhetoric with on-the-bike potential then, no, they were making a misjudgement.

One problem, some seem to think, is that soon Gerdemann lost the ability to distinguish between the two things. Either that or, being intelligent, he realised that he would never live up to his exaggerated billing as a cyclist, but that there was a way to carve out exposure and therefore earnings as the German peloton's unelected spokesperson. Which isn't to say that he immediately stopped performing. In March 2008, indeed, he looked to be closing in on his biggest victory to date at Tirreno-Adriatico when he crashed near the end of the hilly, 26-kilometre time trial to Recanati. X-rays later showed a badly broken femur. Incredibly, he had still got up and finished the time trial in eighth position.

Brian Holm, one of Highroad's *directeurs sportifs* at the time, today answers any questions about Gerdemann's commitment with succinct assertion: 'You don't fall and break your leg in a time trial then get up and finish the thing in the top ten without being a proper bike rider.'

Equally, neither do you reel off victories at the Tour de l'Ain, the Coppa Agostoni and the Deutschland Tour six months later, as Gerdemann did, without having shown immense dedication in your recovery. It was no wonder that, after a lean start to life as a team sponsor, German dairy-goods brand Milram saw Gerdemann as the ideal man to provide some impetus. Milram knew that Gerdemann was under contract, but then they also knew that hadn't stopped him from leaving CSC for T-Mobile.

Sure enough, when they made him what was reportedly an astronomical offer, Gerdemann called Aldag and Bob Stapleton and informed them that he wanted to leave. It wasn't just the money, Gerdemann told the Team Columbia management; Gerolsteiner were being forced out of the sport by doping scandals, T-Mobile had already gone, and Gerdemann felt that the only remaining German elite team, Milram, needed a German rider as their figurehead.

As Aldag puts it: 'Milram were offering to pay him a lot, and he'd got very vocal about anti-doping. He was very clear in the conversation we had about wanting to make a contribution to German cycling. We said okay, but it was a very complicated situation that he was going into. As a bike rider, you have to focus on that part of your job, racing and training, not on saving the sport. We went through the pros and cons and pretty much everything that we said would happen, happened…'

Speaking at the end of that year, with Gerdemann's and his friend Gerald Ciolek's moves to Milram confirmed, Mark Cavendish waxed poetic about how they would be missed.

'I wouldn't just take them back, I'd lasso them back,' Cavendish said. Bob Stapleton, the man who allowed Gerdemann to leave, didn't quite share that view. In interviews at the time, Stapleton showered Ciolek with praise, but was conspicuously blasé about Gerdemann.

'The best part of Linus was releasing him to Milram,' Stapleton reflects waspishly now.

If that sounds severe, it would be harsher still – but tempting – to detect the prophecy in something said by another high-profile American at around the same time. Responding to Gerdemann's comment that Lance Armstrong's comeback was not '100 per cent a good thing for cycling', Armstrong sneered, 'I don't know who the hell Linus Gerdemann is…' Based on Armstrong's next remark – 'He better hope he doesn't get in a breakaway with me because I can still ride hard' – Gerdemann looked in danger of emulating not Ullrich but another of Armstrong's former *bêtes noires*, the Italian Filippo Simeoni.

* * *

Armstrong, however, had posed a good question: who the hell was Linus Gerdemann? Who the hell is he? And would answering that explain why, in retrospect, the day that Gerdemann joined Milram appears to have been the moment when the end began?

In terms of results alone, his two years before the German team folded at the end of 2010 were far from disastrous. An overall win in the 2009 Bayern Rundfahrt, a pair of victories in the

Challenge Majorca and Tirreno-Adriatico the following year, a smattering of top tens... It wasn't that bad, but it just wasn't that good, either. Certainly not for a man who, by then, was one of the higher-earning riders in the professional peloton.

Holm, like others, can only speculate as to what didn't quite work. His affectionate nickname for Gerdemann – Lady Gaga – may tell half the story. But only half. For while the millionaire's lifestyle, the flat that Gerdemann would soon be renting in Monaco, the model girlfriend and expensive clothes reel us towards a familiar stereotype, Holm paints a more textured portrait.

'I always liked Lady Gaga,' the Dane sets out straight away. 'He was a very nice kid, good to work with. He was a diamond. On the bike as well – good climber, could time trial, could sprint... He was what you'd call a really complete rider. But I think he needed someone kicking his ass every now and again, like Aldag did at T-Mobile. That's probably what he didn't get at Milram. For example, quite a few times I'd tell him off about showing up with a dirty bike. It seems like a small thing, but, like I used to tell him, it says something about how you approach your profession and the kind of life you lead away from the team, how much you care. It's important. For sure he would have worked it out eventually, but maybe it got a bit too easy for him at Milram.

'The problem for a lot of these guys comes when

they've got pretty much everything they want out of the sport,' Holm continues. 'They've got money, the car, the pretty girl, the admiration. Then what? Then you have to somehow get the anger back, the fire. Boonen's done it, and Ciolek's had to do it, because he got that kick up the ass, as well. Now Lady Gaga has to do it. Maybe this, ending up without a contract, will be that kick up the backside.'

As for why Gerdemann finds himself in that predicament, jobless six summers after taking the yellow jersey, Holm can only assume that he has priced himself out of a seller's market. That and, possibly, fallen foul of cycling's petty jealousies.

'You know, cycling's pretty conservative,' Holm says. 'The other riders, the guys in your team, might be impressed if you come along with your big house and a good haircut, but meanwhile others will be saying, "Who the hell does he think he is?"'

Gerdemann? A good haircut?

'Well, for a German,' Holm clarifies. 'The girls seem to like it…'

Nygaard, another Dane, agrees that, at various points in his career, Gerdemann has been helped and hindered by his carefully constructed image. Having worked with the German at CSC, Nygaard signed him for Leopard-Trek on the Schleck brothers' and Kim Andersen's advice at the start of 2011.

He disagrees with Bob Stapleton's claim that Gerdemann was 'high maintenance in the extreme', and Aldag's that he was 'very time-consuming'. On the contrary, Nygaard says: 'While quite a few riders were making a fuss about little things like the team-issue suitcases not being ready straight away, Linus was very patient and mature about it. He knew it was a new team, and that there are always teething problems with new teams. He was very sympathetic.'

Gerdemann's main weakness, Nygaard says, is perhaps not his public persona itself, but not realising how it looks through the tint of another person's prejudices.

'I think that maybe people do judge him unfairly, but that he doesn't make allowances for that. He doesn't realise.'

Beyond this problem of perception, Nygaard, like everyone else I speak to, makes only minor criticisms. Gerdemann is not, he says, the most monastically dedicated rider that he has ever met or worked with. By the same token, Nygaard admits, you won't find many slackers in the gym pumping iron after stages of the Tour Down Under, like Gerdemann was in January 2012. He can be scatter-brained – 'If he takes three things into a hotel room, he'll forget two of them,' says Nygaard – but then, equally, Oscar Freire was a world champion at losing things before he won three rainbow jerseys.

On the bike, almost everyone seems to concur, at the right weight and in top form, even now Gerdemann could be a regular winner of races like the Tour of the Basque Country and Tirreno-Adriatico, and perhaps on the outer margins of the top ten in major tours.

The question, then, can only be restated: why doesn't he have a job?

The next to ponder the mystery is one of Gerdemann's closest friends, Ken Sommer, the former marketing director at Leopard-Trek.

'I know that people see him as arrogant,' Sommer says. 'Linus is good-looking and quiet, and that combination often gives people a certain air. They're seen as arrogant. Linus is actually just quite shy and thoughtful, but people look at the glamorous girlfriend, the nice clothes, the fact that he lives in Monaco, and they think he's some kind of international playboy. And you know how the cycling world is – when people have that impression, it spreads to other riders and team managers.

'The other problem,' Sommer continues, 'is that people know Linus was on a big team and on good money before, and they assume they can't afford him. They don't even ask. There's that, and the fact that Linus is clever and won't sign just anything. He'll only go to a team where he has good support, clear goals. He knows what he can do and what he can't do. He's also not desperate – he has a lot of interests outside of cycling. He likes architecture, art. He's a bit different from your average cyclist. Maybe that's another thing that counts against him.'

What Sommer calls 'clever', though, others consider foolhardy or unnecessarily stubborn. Aldag says that, with at least two teams potentially closing at the end of the 2013 season, those that remain will be spoilt for choice. They will take a lot of convincing that a rider with no racing in his legs and no ranking points represents a shrewd investment.

'In my opinion Linus absolutely has to be racing this season,' Aldag says. 'I don't see motivation as a problem. You can look at Linus and say he likes to have nice clothes, a nice car, status symbols, but I'd actually turn that round and see it as a positive thing: he'll know that to sustain that lifestyle he needs to be earning good money, and to earn good money he needs to be riding at a high level.'

Marcel Wüst, Gerdemann's old press attaché at Winfix, is of the same opinion: Gerdemann needs to be racing, and soon, for the same reasons.

'I know Linus earned a shit-load of money at Milram – probably more than I earned in my whole career – but that doesn't last long if you're renting apartments in Monaco and living in Majorca. I've got a place in Majorca, too, and I can assure you it's bloody expensive. He's probably quite a rich man – but he's not an Arab prince with a yacht moored in the harbour. Only if you've got that kind of money will it last for 20 years.

'If I was in Linus's position, I'd have just taken whatever they were offering, maybe with a decent bonus structure and said, "Okay, I'm going to prove myself." It happened to me in 1995 at Le Groupement. They told us a week before the Tour that we weren't going to the race. That was the good news; the bad was that we weren't going to get our wages for June.

'I said, okay, accepted a shitty offer from this tiny Spanish team, Castellblanch, and just took it as an opportunity to prove that I was good enough for a big team. Sure enough, off I went and won three stages of the Vuelta, and that relaunched my career.'

* * *

Contacting and requesting an interview with Linus Gerdemann is today not quite the simple undertaking it once was. Without a team, 'Lady Gaga' is, naturally, also without a press officer. A few years ago, this hurdle would have been overcome with one call to a German colleague, but even the numbers and e-mail addresses in their Filofaxes are out of date.

'I think he might have changed his number when we kept calling him about doping,' says one long-serving, Munich-based Tour reporter gloomily.

I eventually obtain a French mobile number from Sommer, but pinning his friend down proves quite a challenge. After four days of text messages, voice-mails, and a couple of brief conversations to agree a very vaguely convenient time, Gerdemann suddenly vanishes. I assume it's because he's got cold feet, and after four days have given up hope, only for his name to flash suddenly onto my mobile display the following Monday morning. The voice at the other end of the line is surprisingly chirpy and apologetic.

'I'm really sorry. I lost my phone,' he says. 'We can talk now if you like...'

If that was unexpected, the next 40 minutes are also startling. I knew, like everyone else, that Gerdemann was a good talker, but could not have foreseen that he would speak so expansively and clear-sightedly about a situation that to many in his predicament would feel like a nightmare.

Neither, indeed, would I have expected such good humour from someone variously described to us as 'serious', 'not the biggest joker' and – worst of all – 'very German'. The mere mention of those Louis Vuitton suitcases causes cackles at the other end of the phone.

'Oh God, that again! The way people tell that story, it's as though I came with the full set of Louis Vuitton luggage and two butlers. It was one little suitcase! If I count the number of Louis Vuitton suitcases I see now... Everyone's got one!'

If only everything that Gerdemann has experienced, and everything written in the press over the past few years, was as easy to laugh off. Even before his day in yellow in 2007, Gerdemann had been accused of hypocrisy, having trained under the controversial Italian doctor, Luigi Cecchini for a few months at the beginning of 2006. Another former Cecchini client, Jörg Jaksche, tells us he's quite prepared to believe that Cecchini dispensed only advice on training and not illegal medicine.

Nonetheless, Jaksche says: 'I know what went on in teams where Gerdemann rode because I also raced in them. Without knowing for sure either way, I wouldn't put all of my money on Linus Gerdemann never having doped.'

The former president of the German cycling federation, Sylvia Schenk, stated her misgivings even more forcefully in the wake of Gerdemann's yellow jersey-winning ride to Le Grand Bornand in 2007.

'I don't have a very good feeling about Linus Gerdemann,' Schenk said.

If that didn't hurt or deter Gerdemann, he admits now that allegations by the German TV channel ARD at the end of the 2009 season inflicted a lasting wound. The ARD report stated that, in documents seized from the University of Freiburg clinic accused of doping T-Mobile riders, there was evidence of suspicious fluctuations in Gerdemann's red blood cell count.

In the first six months of 2006, it was said, his haemoglobin had been as low as 14.2 and as high as 17.2. While the variation might be explained by illness or dehydration, it could also be the result of doping. Nothing was ever proven – except that it took only five minutes and one inconclusive story to ruin a reputation.

Gerdemann says that his relationship with the German media cooled almost overnight. He changed his phone number and started turning down interviews. He says that he had nothing to hide – rather, it was a case of realising he now had little to gain. Aldag was right: it wasn't his job to save German cycling. He had done his best, and wilfully or not boosted his marketability in the process, but where had it got the sport in his country? Almost nowhere.

'I used to like speaking about anti-doping because I thought it was important and I could make a contribution, but it got to the point where I couldn't see what good it was doing,' Gerdemann says. 'It felt like I'd been sitting on a barstool talking to a German journalist about doping every night for four years, but the conversation wasn't moving forward. The questions were still all the same. Then suddenly they produce a story like the one about my blood values. I tell them, "Okay, let's discuss it. What are these values?" and the journalist says that they can't get the exact figures. I mean, after a while, you just feel like telling them to leave you alone.

'Tony Martin and I were discussing it the other day. I was on a big sports show on German TV, *Sportschau*, twice, and maybe 90 per cent of the questions were about doping. They've had Tyler Hamilton on the same programme, and [former

Spanish pro] Jesus Manzano… But they haven't had Tony, a German world champion, once. I'm a pretty patient guy, but you get sick of it, like you get sick of seeing dopers coming back into the sport as though nothing's happened, when you're sitting there without a contract.'

Although he insists that he's had low moments over the past few months, Gerdemann is more sanguine now. He'll keep training, keep looking for a team, keep hoping, he says, but at the same time he is mentally prepared for the doomsday scenario of retirement at age 30. He doesn't yet know what he would do but he has a few ideas. Maybe a business or economics degree. Maybe something in cycling, 'because I do still love the sport'.

Whatever it is, his friend Ken Sommer says – and everyone we ask agrees – Linus Gerdemann will do just fine.

Nevertheless, if it does come to that, we'll be forced to surmise that his career will have played out on a riff of regret – if not his, then ours. It is clear from Linus Gerdemann's own synopsis that he regards himself as a child of his time, his fortunes intimately tied to that era's vicissitudes.

'It's been a roller-coaster,' he reflects with a sigh. 'I took the yellow jersey, lost it to Michael Rasmussen, and the same day my team-mate, Patrik Sinkewitz was positive. Then the next year I won the Deutschland Tour, my biggest win yet, and straight away Stefan

Schumacher and Bernhard Kohl tested positive and that story was all over the news. That's the way it seems to have gone in my career: every time something good happened, something bad came straight afterwards.'

He has no pretensions of martyrdom, no real belief, ultimately, that voicing opinions about drugs has cost him his livelihood. In that respect, no, he is not another Filippo Simeoni. Even so, Linus Gerdemann is trying to say – and is perfectly entitled to say – that it seems perverse that he of all people now finds himself on the outside looking in.

For that, of course, he can also blame both his own unwillingness to compromise, what he calls his 'principles', and the team managers who didn't take him at his over-inflated asking price. Apparently they also realised, as even Gerdemann's friend Ken Sommer concedes, that 'he just wasn't as good as was first made out'.

It's a life-lesson that confronts us all at some point – just not one Linus Gerdemann or Germany could have foreseen only six summers ago.

Daniel Friebe began writing on pro cycling midway through a Modern Languages degree at University College London in October 2000. He has covered 12 Tours de France and reported every major race on the UCI calendar, plus a few minor ones, including his favourite, the Volta a Portugal. Now *Procycling*'s roving European Editor, he is the author of *Eddy Merckx: The Cannibal* and *Mountain High* and collaborated with Mark Cavendish on his autobiographical *Boy Racer*.

7

Since 1994, **Jeremy Whittle** has returned to the Tour de France each year to cover the race. The 2013 edition will be his 20th.

Following the Tour can be a rollercoaster ride, both physically and emotionally, particularly during an era blighted by scandal.

But, he concludes, despite everything, the Tour is still the Tour and it has an intoxicating charm no other event can match.

ÇA M'EST ÉGAL

BY JEREMY WHITTLE

For a long time, I dreamed of being part of the Tour de France. But it can also become a nightmare. I've had my bad dream a few times now.

The house is somewhere in London, in the old East End – not the gentrified post-Olympic East End of flower shops, macchiatos, cupcakes and Tracey Emin – but the evil, malevolent East End of dark Victorian streets, of failing sodium lights and gloomy subways, of glowering, shattered tower blocks.

I'm asleep in an end-of-terrace house on a freezing winter night. I wake up, it's hot and I can smell smoke. I slide out of bed and hear rumbling, as if a tube train is running beneath the house. As I walk downstairs, smoke fills my nostrils and the atmosphere is acrid, choking. I open the front door. A blast of icy air cuts through me and fills the hall. Barefoot, I step out into the street.

Through the charred basement window of the flat below, I see flames flickering, rising in rage.

I peer in and see the room is burning, the walls are blackened, sweating, calcified.

A dog, his eyes bulging, his tongue lolling, pads unsteadily across the pulsating room, towards me, framed by the broiling heat.

Horrified, I stumble down the basement steps to the sash window and begin scrabbling at the red-hot charred wood, in desperation.

The dog stands, staring at me, and, engulfed by the inferno, howls in agony.

I wake up in tears.

I talked to an expert about the dream.

He said it had been caused by trauma, or unresolved conflict. I told him there had been a few of those over the years. Maybe it was about shame or perhaps a sense of profound guilt. But to me it was very evident what it all meant.

Surely, it's obvious.

The dog is Lance Armstrong.

Or then again, maybe he's me. The fact that I can't decide makes it even funnier.

But then he could be others – Marco Pantani, Frank Vandenbroucke, or possibly Filippo Simeoni. Maybe it's Jesus Manzano, Floyd Landis or Jörg Jaksche... You remember Jörg, right? No, no – the dog's not Jörg I don't think – he's doing okay these days. He got out in time.

You see, that's what you get for 20 years on the Tour de France: shot by both sides and a bad night's sleep... So, as LA would say, if I hate it so goddamn much, why do I keep going back...?

* * *

I remember July 1994. I remember my first Tour. I loved my first Tour.

I remember the Peugeot 504 with worn, melted, non-existent brakes barrelling through the hills outside Morzine.

I remember the crippling dinner-table conversations as my faltering French succumbed to its limitations and I retreated into defeated semi-inebriated isolation.

I remember a policeman stepping into the peloton to take a photograph in Armentières and wrecking careers as he did so. I remember the Tour's director, Jean-Marie Leblanc, angrily denying that a French policeman would do such a thing, even as the TV screen behind him lovingly replayed the same image, over and over, of a gendarme pressing the shutter of an Instamatic.

And I remember a French colleague – let's call him C – a real lothario weary of cycling and weary of the world, facing up to imminent divorce by skirt-chasing from the Pyrenees to Paris.

I remember that in 1994 John Lelangue was the autocratic head of the Tour's press service. Even now, John is still doing his best to manage the media, in his role directing BMC. Lelangue also directed Phonak, sponsors of Santiago Botero, Tyler Hamilton and Floyd Landis.

I remember that year's big fish: Piotr Ugrumov, Miguel Indurain, Pantani, Bjarne Riis. At least I think I do, even if it's like a flashback from a long-forgotten Oliver Stone movie. I think they were there in 1994, phantoms from a distant era, in their loud kit, all racing caps, no helmets, camper vans, no buses, endlessly pounding the big ring in their bug-eyed sunglasses.

I know *He* was there – the Texan, that is. I was buddying up to him back then, when he was the upstart and I was the newbie, both of us in our own ways just burnin' up with the need to kick ass. Most of the time he was his own worst enemy, winding himself up with the Italians, mocking the French, looking to Big Sean, his room-mate, for guidance.

It all started in appropriately crazed fashion in a hotel car park in Lille. I stood in the lobby watching as a Gan team car pulled dramatically to a screeching halt, Greg LeMond jumped out, unzipped and took a leak behind a tree in the hotel garden.

Moments later, a British press car slid into some street furniture, the driver frothing with excitement at the mere hint of Chris Boardman's presence. I was goggle-eyed at the madness of it all, utterly naïve and ignorant of what I was really getting myself into.

There were no British riders back then – well, only 'Big Sean' Yates and Boardman. There were no British 'colleagues,' to speak of, in the press room – or at least the ones that were there were usually so disdainful of Tour virgins, so painfully desperate to hide their Britishness, that they were strangers to me.

So I sat among the French, biding my time, on the right-hand side of the back seat of the Peugeot for three weeks, my right arm reddening, browning, then finally curing like serrano, as we kerb-crawled south from Lille – via Dover, Brighton and Portsmouth – eventually, mercifully, out of Jean-Marie Leblanc's endless hours of *Nordiste* bread-basket flatness, to the beautiful mysterious mountains.

Only one rider could win that year, a dead-eyed, mono-browed, lop-sided Spaniard, churning his way across Europe, unrelenting, unsmiling. Indurain was unmoved by the terrain; flat roads, time trials, *moyenne montagne*, the thin air of the Tourmalet and Galibier – it was all the same to him.

His joyless run of victories – 1994 was his fourth – left only scraps for the others. Boardman and Yates knew how to seize the day, and both took the race lead in the first week. Boardman's record-breaking prologue victory baffled and dumbfounded the French, such was its technological and physiological advancement.

Unfortunately, his level of know-how even baffled his own team-mates and they collapsed in the team time trial, ending Boardman's time in yellow. His ambitions crumbled en route to the Eurotunnel and the gulf between his professionalism and that of his sponsor was laid bare for all to see.

To make up for it, he attacked on the stage through Kent and Sussex, so hyped that he was bouncing off the walls in Brighton, punching the air even though he didn't win the stage.

Nose pressed against the crowd barriers on Brighton seafront, the teenage David Millar drank it all in and stoked his dreams.

The next morning in Portsmouth, Armstrong held court in the start village.

'How was the transfer over here last night?' I asked as we sipped bad coffee.

'Slooow man,' he said. 'It was painful. You don't even have any highways here.'

Big Sean got the yellow jersey when we got back to France, within hours of Boardman losing it. When he did, I got so excited that I dared ask a question in English at the post-race press conference. But I got shouted down, because these were the days when the language of cycling was French, when the home nation still believed it could win, when you got told off for asking questions of a Brit in your mother tongue.

The grimmest feature of that first Tour were the hotel rooms, a series of filthy and forgotten flea-pits with fag-burnt sheets, where rooms were often rented by the hour.

I can still remember the worst one – where we had inter-connecting rooms and I was forced to listen to C's guttural exclamations of ecstasy after yet another local Madame had succumbed to his promise of a start-village introduction to Richard Virenque.

Now everybody speaks English and stays in an Ibis, Novotel, Mercure, Etap, or Formule 1, where the bar is always open late and the wi-fi is on tap. Only the most fogeyish *suiveur* still seeks out an *auberge* where they bake their own bread and make their own *confiture*.

It was somewhere in the middle of that year's race, that my infatuation was consecrated. On a baking hot afternoon – down towards Brive perhaps – the French let me drive the Peugeot, *in* the race, for the first time. They always drove *in* the race – that is, among the teams cars and riders. Always.

After all, you couldn't *properly* understand the Tour just from tearing down the *autoroute* to the press room, grabbing a *cornichon* and watching the telly. Goddet and Lévitan didn't take the *hors course*, did they?

C and his colleagues, family and friends lived the Tour as Groundhog Day. Every morning, we would speed away down the stage route, ahead of the start, slaloming through the publicity caravan, then stopping for the ritualistic bad-coffee-and-fag break.

Then, 25 minutes later, after watching the *caravane publicitaire* roll past from a pavement table, we'd head out, onto the route again, race radio crackling – '*B-a-a-nesto, B-a-a-nesto, arriere du peloton…*' – trundling along in the sun, at 30 kilometres an hour, waiting for the breakaway to appear in our rear-view mirror.

Only this time, C had stubbed out his Marlboro, tossed me the keys, nodded approvingly and climbed into the passenger seat.

While C snoozed, we rolled gently through the bucolic landscape so typical of the Tour, as it meandered through *la France profonde*. Hay wains, shuttered mansions, sawdust cafes, trickling fountains, tumble down garages, burnt, putty-coloured fields stretching to the horizon.

After a while, the *Garde Républicaine*'s outriders became more frequent, the photographers began overtaking us, until finally, shimmering in the heat haze behind us, I spotted the glinting, glittering spokes, then the red Fiat, the race director's car, and finally the swaying flotilla of roof racks, following in the breakaway's wake.

We pulled over and watched them pass, before dropping into the convoy behind them, jostling for position with the VIPs and *suiveurs*, my heart pounding as much as if I'd been on the bike myself. It was a coming of age.

* * *

I don't drive in the race much these days, at least not since Johnny Hoogerland and Juan Antonio Flecha got sent flying by a guest car two years ago. There are too many cars and motorbikes buzzing the riders already – who needs another press car cluttering up the climbs?

Apart from anything else there's not enough time. In 1994, there were only newspapers and magazines to write for. Not any more. My old boss was always crapping on about the coming of the internet, but back then he could never get his modem to work.

Some days, though, driving in the race is still essential – because there are often days when the back of the race is more interesting than the front, when the fight to survive is more enthralling than the battle to win.

Every now and then, when the deadlines, bad food, tetchy stars and media handlers get too oppressive, it's good to dip into the back of the race, as if returning to the source. On the final climb at the end of a big mountain stage, find the last man on the road – there you will see the essence of the Tour in that rider's face.

But then covering the Tour is not 'a job' – it's like taking holy orders, even down to the blind faith. Like the best or worst relationships, it evolves and changes; it is fluid, not static.

It's a grand passion, a commitment, a relationship. And it can be a very long time away from home if you want to get out. I learned that much in 1998.

Since that first Tour the audience has changed, grown up, become massively knowledgable. The sport has changed too, the rewards multiplying and the pressures increasing. There are new demands now – corporate, ethical, commercial.

Once, aghast at the scale of the Tour, bewitched by the myths and legends that had become so vivid over the years, we applauded the peloton regardless, just for daring to tackle the damn thing. A long list of cultural changes – the internet, live TV coverage, Twitter, cheap flights – have changed that perception. Now we reserve the right to judge, to question – to demand transparency.

Since Lance Armstrong, lauded for so long as the greatest champion in the history of the Tour, better even than Merckx, Hinault or Anquetil, was so totally unmasked, the fight for our heart and soul has been fierce.

But where are we now? Who can we trust? Everybody and nobody?

The truth is, I don't know.

I can't adopt a position where Paul Kimmage is unquestioningly right, or David Walsh is judge and jury, where Lance is the personification of evil or Pat McQuaid is willfully bad. These are simple and convenient positions to adopt. Life is never that black and white. People are never that black and white.

Last year I thought zero tolerance, certainly in terms of young riders, was misplaced. More recently, post-Fuentes trial, it has started to make more sense. The dire prospect of Manolo Saiz, or Johan Bruyneel, ever being able to again direct a professional team has complicated that debate.

And I find it surreal, listening to the riders who for years praised Armstrong, lionised him, celebrated his comeback, who claimed to have learned a lot from him on dealing with the media, who said they were fans – to hear those riders now moaning about negative coverage of the sport. Now that *is* funny.

Many of them now claim, like the UCI, to be shocked, stunned, betrayed, angered by Lance's legacy, by the questions they now have to contend with. All of which makes them sound pretty dumb to me.

Thing is, by the time he made his comeback in 2009, we all knew *really* – didn't we?

Christophe Bassons knew, Hamilton knew, Jaksche knew, and, by then, an army of us knew. I mean, even I knew – *so how come they didn't?*

* * *

Mostly, it's the little things, the people and places, that stay in your mind.

Beers and a barbecue at sunset at Luz Ardiden, Marc Lavoine singing *Ça m'est égal* every morning, day-in, day-out, on M6, late night flaming Drambuie-chasing in Carcasonne; Johan Bruyneel proudly telling me that it takes panache – not doping, you understand but panache – to win seven Tours, Luuc Eisenga reaching out of a Rabobank team car and

lending me his phone on the morning of 7/7, when
the terrors of the Tube bombings cut me off from
my family.

Some years – Carlos Sastre's Tour win in 2008
springs to mind – are forgettable, while others
resonate. Patrick Lefevere, bemused by the media
laying siege to the hotel that both teams were billeted
in, appearing like a ghost in the wooded garden of
the Mapei hotel on the night in July 1998 that the
Festina team fell apart.

Armstrong and Walsh circling each other in 2001
in Pau, in an electric press conference that exposed
the American for the Godfather he had become; Jan
Ullrich, almost blacking out with exhaustion and
hypothermia at Les Deux Alpes, after Marco Pantani
had laid waste to his hopes of a second Tour win.

The Schleck brothers wandering aimlessly
through the crowds massing around the Grenoble
time trial finish, adjusting to yet another Big Miss
after Cadel Evans sealed victory; and last year, 15
summers after Festina, the questioning of Sky, the
rage of soon-to-be Sir Bradley; the media frenzy in
Pau around the RadioShack hotel at dusk – just like
the media frenzies in 1998 and 2006 – when Frank
Schleck fell from his perch.

The Tour is complex, grandiose, overblown. It is
wayward, beautiful, sordid and sometimes demented.
It is an anachronism, struggling to come to terms
with corporate commitments, lurching uncertainly to

meet new ethical expectations. In truth, perhaps we shouldn't expect too much of an event that has more in common with the ritual cruelty of the Coliseum than chess on wheels.

The riders come and go, the scandals come and go, the sponsors come and go. The race remains, the landscape unchanged and timeless, the seasons weathering rural roads that are baked in the summer, frozen and cracked through the winter.

In the end, though, it's just a bike race. At the moment, the British are doing well, like the French, Italians, Belgians and Spaniards before them. It will pass and, soon enough, other champions will be along to replace them. Try and keep hold of that thought, when, as they inevitably will, all the intoxications of the Tour, the sound and the fury, once again get too much.

Jeremy Whittle is cycling correspondent to *The Times*, author of *Bad Blood: The secret life of the Tour de France,*' and collaborator with David Millar on *Racing Through the Dark*. A founding editor of *procycling* magazine, he has written about sport, particularly European cycling, since 1994 and has covered 19 Tours de France.

8

William Fotheringham explores the legacy of Cyrille Guimard, the French directeur sportif who guided Lucien Van Impe, Bernard Hinault and Laurent Fignon to victory at the Tour.

Guimard also arguably discovered Greg LeMond, who went on to win the race three times.

The *directeur sportif* used to be king. Guimard was a combination of talent-spotter, master-tactician, motivator and dictator. With seven Tour wins, he could stake a claim to be the best ever.

NAPOLEON

BY WILLIAM FOTHERINGHAM

It's a given that the greatest rider in the history of the Tour de France is Eddy Merckx, and the title of most influential *directeur sportif* is equally clear-cut. Cyrille Guimard now cuts a diminished figure when he turns up on the Tour, making low-key appearances as a radio consultant. The buoyant curls that were his trademark in the 1970s and 1980s are a little flat and grey now, the empire built by 'Napoleon' has disappeared, but the statistics are as trenchant on his behalf as they are for Merckx.

Who could argue with seven Tour wins in eight years between 1976 and 1984, with three different riders directly under his command? He won the Tour with Lucien Van Impe, Bernard Hinault, and the late Laurent Fignon.

Hinault and Guimard's other celebrated protégé, Greg LeMond, added a further four between 1985 and 1990 after leaving him; like Hinault, the American was formed in the Guimard stable. Eleven of the first 78 Tours: that's quite a record for a man now working with Roubaix-Lille-Métropole, a small team ranked in the UCI Continental division, today. Of the top teams currently in cycling, you can see Team Sky, in particular, working along similar lines to those which proved so successful for 'Napoleon' many years ago.

The only other manager remotely in Guimard's bracket is José-Miguel Echavarri, founder of the squad that morphed from Reynolds into Banesto, then Illes Baleares and are now Movistar, and who won six Tours between 1988 and 1995 with Pedro Delgado and Miguel Indurain.

In 1984, I spent my first year racing in France. I was a teenage bike rider who devoured every scrap of information and every minute of live television, so I was lucky enough to follow the edition of the Tour that was the *chef d'oeuvre* of Guimard's time in the driving seat at the squad which bore the colours of Gitane, then Renault, then Système-U and finally Castorama. That year, I watched at the roadside between Cergy-Pontoise and Alençon, as first a three-man break rode past, then, an eternity later, an idling peloton. In the move was Vincent Barteau, a young pro with Renault who was given almost 20 minutes by the 'heads' of the race, and who would hold the *maillot jaune* from Alençon to the Alps, two weeks later.

That move was a key element in the head-to-head that dominated the race: Fignon, then at his ephemeral best, against Hinault, on the road back

to the top after a knee operation. It pitted Fignon
and Guimard's Renault against the new kids on the
block: the La Vie Claire squad that had been formed
over the winter by Hinault and the decidedly louche
magnate Bernard Tapie. Fignon and Guimard won
by a country mile, the Parisian taking the overall
classification and five stages, his team-mates adding
another five between them. Few teams have dominated the Tour to that extent.

'Fignon just played with Hinault,' recalls Robert
Millar, who finished fourth that year. 'For the rest of
us it was a case of picking up what the pair of them
left behind.'

'It was a strong team, a young team, and we won
one day out of two,' says Marc Madiot, back then
a starlet at Renault, now *directeur sportif* at Française
des Jeux. 'We'd all begun our careers at Renault, and
there was a strong "house spirit".'

'Guimard was really smart,' LeMond told the
writer Richard Moore in his account of the 1986
Tour, *Slaying the Badger*. 'I don't believe any really great
cyclists make good coaches, because their ego gets
in the way. They don't recognise all the inputs. But,
for Guimard, one of his riders winning was like him
winning. He was not super-talented as a rider, but he
was really tactical. As a rider he was a sprinter and I
think the sprinters make the good coaches: they have
to survive, to read the race, conserve energy.'

'He was the young guy with the best brain at the

time,' says the French writer Jean-François Quénet. 'He's out of date now, but back then he changed the way *directeurs sportifs* work.'

There were times, as we sat in front of the television at my club team manager's place that July, when we got bored of Renault's domination, of the days when the peloton seemed powerless to match the riders in yellow and black, although that was quickly forgotten when our best rider, Thierry Marie, signed with Guimard a few weeks later. That was the highlight of my boss's career, perhaps of his life — like a manager running a non-league club who spots a player and has him signed straight into the first team at Manchester United. It didn't get any better for Robert Vogt, a roofer from deepest Normandy, than putting a rider in the best team in the world, and it's now clear that for French cycling it has never got any better than the Hinault-Fignon Tour, the last *Grande Boucle* that was *une affaire franco-française*: a wholly French matter.

* * *

It's a given that professional sport is a high-octane occupation: the love-ins and the fallings-out are hardly surprising. You raise your eyebrows when you realise that Cyrille Guimard had rancorous splits with all his best riders, until you ask yourself this: how many star cyclists eventually fall out with their *directeurs sportifs*?

Those that remain friends are the exception, and it's probably the same throughout all professional sports. You put together two highly competitive individuals and mix in a liberal smattering of sponsor pressure, high economic rewards and then pepper it with the inexorable law of aging that means all sportsmen have a limited shelf-life. The bust-ups are inevitable.

'You love Guimard or you detest him,' said Hinault. Fignon is coruscating about Guimard in his memoirs, Hinault a little less so; Marc Madiot and he were at loggerheads for years – there has been a rapprochement more recently – but that has a perfect logic to it.

Guimard had a character which lent itself to the extremes of his chosen sport. His was a classic upbringing in rural France – his grandparents' farm was close to where Nantes airport now stands – and a classic tale of the impoverished lad who fights to race his bike.

He made himself ill working in his early teens to earn the money to pay for his first bike; recalled in his memoirs that he had 'no shoes, no shorts, no jersey' and devised a variety of ruses to make money to finance his racing, siphoning cash from his lunch money at school and getting his friends to pretend they were going to the cinema, then 'reclaiming' the cash. He was an individualist, who annoyed his workmates in a Nantes shipyard by getting through their tasks as quickly as he could so that he could rest before training, rather than letting the work fill the available hours.

As a young professional in 1968 it took only weeks for Guimard to earn his first nickname – *'Petit Chef'*, or 'Little Boss', which morphed later into Napoleon. He earned the monicker for being the kind of young pro who tells his team-mates he is going to win and they must therefore work for him. Fortunately for him, he won early, and he won often. He rapidly earned a reputation for speaking his mind, whether it was with his more seasoned team-mates when racing, or with his team's wheel supplier over kit he felt could and should be better. Like Eddy Merckx, he was nearly killed in a crash in September 1969: the collision with a car as he left a hotel in Nantes to go training left him in a coma for two days, resulted in permanent memory loss, and eventually ended his career.

Guimard's battle with Merckx in the 1972 Tour drew him plaudits in France for his tenacity, his apparent unwillingness to accept that The Cannibal's victory was inevitable, but it ended in bitter tears, with tendinitis in his knees forcing him out of the race with three days remaining and with second place overall and victory in the points competition seemingly assured.

The scene when he appeared on the final podium in Paris, and Merckx handed him the green jersey which had just been pulled over his shoulders, was as emotional as you would expect. Ironically, tendinitis would have a heavy bearing on the careers of both his best protégés, Laurent Fignon and Bernard Hinault.

The next three years were spent trying to race in spite of the knee problems – which were eventually linked back to that crash in 1969 – but by 1975, Guimard knew that the game was up. He had begun coaching studies at just 17, and had been 'directing' his teams on the road as a professional, so his future career was obvious.

He wasn't the first choice at the Gitane team to replace Jacques Anquetil's former henchman Jean Stablinski as *directeur sportif*, but the job was given to him after some intense lobbying by an old acquaintance, Jose Alvarez, who was one of Gitane's leading dealers, and a major player in the French bike industry.

* * *

Before his appointment, Guimard had already made a key move, and probably the most important one of his entire career. He had secured a verbal agreement with a pugnacious young professional called Bernard Hinault, another Breton, albeit from the north coast.

Hinault was already riding for Gitane, but had a disastrously poor relationship with Stablinski, and

was about to move to the Gan-Mercier team run by
the more empathetic Louis Caput, where he would
have joined the legendary Raymond Poulidor.

But Guimard had had his eyes on Hinault for
a while, and had been offering him the occasional
nugget of advice; as a result, Hinault agreed to stay.
It was a classic *Sliding Doors* moment. Hinault himself
was convinced his career would have taken a completely different turn had he moved on instead of
staying with Renault and Guimard.

Critically, with Hinault, as with LeMond later,
Guimard established a clear-cut career plan, something which was rare at the time. Hinault would stay
out of the Tour de France for several years.

Stablinski had wanted him in the Tour – to get
publicity by livening up the early stages – in 1975;
under Guimard, 1976 would be focused on French
events which were realistic goals – Paris-Camembert,
the Circuit de la Sarthe and so on – while the next
year would see Hinault move to the Classics and the
Dauphiné Libéré before, eventually, being unleashed
on the Tour in 1978. The rest was history.

Guimard had become a *directeur sportif* at 28 –
the age when most professional cyclists hit their
prime. The energy and passion which should
have gone into winning in his own right went into
winning by proxy. It seems incredible now, but in his
memoirs Guimard states that he specified he should
be paid the French minimum wage in his first year as

manager of Gitane – 1976 – on the grounds that his qualities were unproven.

That changed rapidly. He cajoled the star rider he had inherited at Gitane, Lucien Van Impe, into winning that year's Tour. That entailed a tactical masterstroke whereby – having gained the approval of Gitane's directors first – Guimard persuaded the French journeyman Raymond Delisle, who rode for Peugeot, to attack and relieve Van Impe of the yellow jersey, to take the pressure off the relatively weak Gitane team. At the time it seemed incomprehensible to most of the Tour caravan, and the official Tour history still records it as a major upset.

Van Impe wasn't exactly willing for this to happen either – his wife had just turned up on the race so he didn't want to lose the jersey in front of her. He then had to be strong-armed into making the vital attack to regain the jersey a couple of days later on the stage to Pla d'Adet.

Guimard knew that only a long-range attack, early in the stage, would gain the necessary time; the plan was agreed, but Van Impe did not have the confidence to execute it.

It is common knowledge that Guimard only made Van Impe attack by driving up into the peloton and virtually threatening him, but it took even more to get him to follow through with his effort once the gap had been opened.

Initially, Van Impe was cruising some 30 seconds

off the front of the peloton; he needed to press on, but, because team cars were not allowed into a gap of less than a minute between a break and the peloton, Guimard could not drive up and give him an earbashing. To do that, he had to persuade an old friend, Albert Bouvet, who 'regulated' the Tour's internal traffic, to tell the race director, Félix Lévitan, that the gap was over a minute.

The white lie worked; Guimard's attempt to get Van Impe moving didn't. 'Too far, too hard,' was the gist of the Belgian's response. The final throw of the dice for the team manager was to ask a car-full of Belgian journalists, who had followed Guimard past the bunch to get a closer look at the action, to persuade their man that he would lose the Tour if he didn't press on the pedals.

It now seems an amusing episode from a smaller, more intimate race than the Tour is today, but it worked. Van Impe won the stage and the Tour, in spite of his innate conservatism.

The Belgian left Gitane at the end of the season, mainly because, with Hinault in the wings, Guimard had no particular need of him but also because the Belgian's individualism didn't fit with the team 'Napoleon' wanted to forge.

Key to that was the revolutionary pay structure he devised for Gitane: the 'Guimard system' was one of salaries based on results, not for the individual rider, but for the team, based on a complicated formula: the role the rider had played in the win, and the significance of the win for the team and the rider. So if Hinault won a small race, he didn't get a pay increase; if a lesser rider did, his salary went up. That in turn created an incentive for the leaders to help their team-mates win smaller events, which in turn forged team spirit. Similarly, when prospective new professionals were brought to train with the team at training camps, it was only partly to see how they performed: the goal was to see what the team made of them, the goal being to keep the squad as a tight-knit unit.

* * *

The battle to keep Hinault out of the 1977 Tour was a tough one, as the newspaper *L'Equipe* – then both organiser and sponsor – ran a campaign to force France's new star to ride after a spectacular early season in which he won both Ghent-Wevelgem and Liège-Bastogne-Liège, and added the Dauphiné Libéré stage race, a few weeks before the Tour.

But Guimard's move was utterly vindicated when Hinault dominated both the 1978 and 1979 Tours. The latter, in particular, was a race which showed Hinault at his best, losing time early on to Joop Zoetemelk, then regaining the initiative by waging a guerilla war through the middle part of the race.

Theirs appears to have been the classic symbiotic

rider-coach relationship – Mark Cavendish and Rod Ellingworth would be a good parallel today – with both men growing into the roles, each feeding off the other's thirst for knowledge. Both seem to acknowledge that they were more dependent on the other than was healthy in the long-term – but that is the pattern.

There was a twist, however, and an important one given Hinault's macho character: they had raced together. Indeed, when Guimard began his stint at Gitane, he had just finished fourth in the world cyclo-cross championships, which meant he was able to rip his riders' legs off at their first training camp. Hinault had just taken several months off after the birth of his and his wife Martine's son Mickael; Guimard clearly realised the best way to motivate his man was not to remonstrate with him for a lack of professionalism, but to ride past him up the climbs, blowing out his cheeks to illustrate how much weight his protégé had put on.

'If he had taken it badly, I might have given up cycling for good,' said Hinault. Similarly, there was no hair-drying when Hinault led team members on a lengthy drinking session at the 1981 Tour de l'Armor (an episode told in loving detail by Fignon). Guimard sat back and simply expected the riders to perform in spite of their hangovers. Which they did.

However, Guimard clearly knew when to apply the disciplinary brakes to his fiery star. The tone was

set at Hinault's first training camp with Guimard,
when he came down ten minutes late for a ride.
Guimard remonstrated, and Hinault replied, 'This
isn't the army you know,' only to have it explained to
him that being late wasn't just about him, but about
his team-mates who had to wait: a classic case of the
'do as you would be done by' argument.

Early in 1977, when Hinault simply disappeared
from the Tour of Flanders because he wasn't in the
mood for riding, Guimard had no hesitation in sending him a registered letter containing a warning about
his conduct. During the 1978 Tour, it was hardly
surprising that Hinault's role in the riders' 'strike' at
Valence d'Agen – when he led the peloton's protest
over early stage starts – played on his mind, and it
took Guimard to refocus him. As well as the odd
kick in the backside, Hinault needed guidance in how
to race.

'Before, I had no idea how to gauge my efforts,' he
admitted. Rather than following every move, Hinault
was taught the virtue of patience: the need to make
one effort, when it really mattered, and make sure
that it counted.

With the support of Hinault, Guimard is credited
with breaking the system that had dominated professional cycling since the 1950s, whereby 'managers'
would arrange appearance contracts for the riders,
who earned the bulk of their money from criteriums
and track meetings. French cycling was dominated

by two such middlemen: Daniel Dousset, who had managed Jacques Anquetil, and Roger Piel, whose roster was headed by Raymond Poulidor. Guimard wanted control of his riders' programmes, so that he knew who was racing where and when, and having 'managers' arrange a large part of their calendar in August and September got in the way of that.

So he negotiated directly with the race organisers to cut out the middlemen, to enable more of his team to get contracts; subsequently, according to Hinault, the organisers and riders worked together on the calendar, aiming to group the races geographically, and they collaborated over aspects such as the safety and the toughness of criterium courses.

Those who smile at the Sky philosophy of 'marginal gains' can be assured that there is nothing new in this. Guimard was one of those who tried this approach many years ago.

'He was the first *directeur sportif* to introduce periodisation,' says Quénet. 'Before, it was "train and race as much as I want you to", but he reduced the days of racing and got his riders to work towards real goals.' Hence, probably, something Fignon noted: the lack of pressure early in the year, the confidence that the wins would come. Which, of course, they did.

On the 'marginal gains' side, Guimard had a major boost when Gitane was taken over by the Renault conglomerate in 1978, at which point the team ceased to be Gitane-Campagnolo and became

Renault-Gitane. Renault had the same philosophy
with their cycle company as with the Formula One
team led by Alain Prost and René Arnoux; research
and development in competition was a key part of
innovation for the consumer market. But it wasn't
just about making the bikes more aerodynamic,
which was the major change most cycling fans saw
from 1979 onwards thanks to Guimard's collabora-
tion with a former Renault engineer Armel André.

The 'Guimard position', adopted by the
riders who went through Renault's biomechanics
programme, was radically different: whereas for years
riders had been hunched over their bikes, and, to cite
Robert Millar, an 11-centimetre stem was a curiosity,
Guimard's riders were stretched forwards, their backs
flat, the stem at least 13 centimetres, the cranks a
massive 180 millimetres to produce more power –
although the record of knee injuries among
Guimard's protégés suggests this wasn't always in
their best interests. All this at a time when most
riders in most teams simply rode what they were
doled out after giving their *directeur sportif* a frame
size. The biomechanics, the aerodynamics, the trips
to the wind tunnels: these weren't just for the leaders,
but for the whole team.

There was the moment in the 1979 Tour when
Renault turned up for a team time trial – a critical
element in that race and the 1980 event, both of
which had two such stages – to find the team van

stuffed with aerodynamic 'Delta' bikes. (Thirty-three years on, Great Britain cycling's head of 'marginal gains' told me how critical it is to roll out key bits of kit at key times. Again, nothing new.)

Guimard's philosophy was that if a team were to win the Tour, as much attention needed to be paid to the riders who were to look after the leader as the leader himself.

'Back then, team riders weren't always treated particularly well when it came to salaries, bonuses, dividing up prize money, or criterium contracts, but Guimard was perfect in that area, it was a bit new and it made a massive difference,' says Madiot.

Similarly, Hinault recalled how Renault were the first team to have a dedicated team bus, a dozen years before the PDM squad brought their 'Black Maria' to races. The Renault vehicle had 15 seats up front for the riders, which could be converted into couchettes for long transfers, while in the back was a space for the mechanics' kit and the team bikes.

* * *

By 1980, Guimard's relationship with Hinault was changing. That was inevitable: having grown together, their needs had altered. Guimard was already aware of the need for renewal, and his mind was no doubt focused by Hinault's withdrawal from the 1980 Tour with a knee injury; Hinault was maturing, becoming less willing to conform as his horizons broadened.

The arrival of Laurent Fignon changed the relationship again; as when Hinault succeeded Van Impe, Guimard had options. In his memoirs – which I translated into English under the title '*We were young and carefree*' – Fignon paints an entertaining picture of both Hinault and Guimard, extreme characters both: the alternately grouchy and all too human 'Badger', the cerebral and highly cautious 'Napoleon'.

Guimard's Renault was, wrote Fignon, 'the cycling equivalent of Oxbridge', crammed with the best kit, the best ideas, home to a group of ambitious youngsters such as Madiot – who had connections with Guimard going back to when he was a junior – Pascal Jules, and Martial Gayant alongside the old guard centred on Hinault.

Madiot describes his old mentor as a man who would place his confidence in young riders more readily than most managers, but, for Fignon, Guimard was an enigmatic figure, a man who liked to make an impression.

'When he spoke, it was as if a century of accumulated knowledge was coming out of his mind.'

He approaches Fignon midway through his last season as an amateur and offers the following pearl of wisdom before a time trial: 'Start quickly, accelerate in the middle, and finish flat out.'

'Bizarre,' thinks the young upstart.

The reasons for the breakdown between Hinault and Guimard are complex: the sacking of Hinault's cousin, René, who worked for Renault, was one factor; Guimard's perception his 'badger' needed a little baiting to provoke him into action may have been another. But more important, it seems, was the matter of control. Hinault, as he grew older, wanted more input, more insight into the workings of the team; Guimard seems to have felt threatened.

Something not dissimilar would happen with Fignon, but with more bitterness, because their working relationship was far, far closer.

Both Fignon and Hinault felt that the relationship took a long time to dissolve; Hinault says it was not the same after his first knee injury in 1980 – 'Cyrille wanted to do everything his way; the rider had only to pedal and keep his mouth shut' – and deteriorated until he left the team in 1983. By now Hinault had won four Tours and Tapie was beckoning as he recovered from a second attack of tendinitis, which took him off the treadmill of competition and finally gave him time for reflection.

In August that year, he told Renault it was him or their *directeur sportif*, but there was little doubt who they would choose, with Fignon having won the Tour at his first attempt a few weeks earlier. Again, Guimard's psychology was masterly; Fignon was made co-leader with Madiot, and given the target of finishing in the top ten and winning a stage, so the pressure was kept off him. When he took the yellow jersey after Pascal Simon's withdrawal with a broken shoulder, the situation was the same as it had been with Van Impe in 1976 and Hinault in 1978: a rider had to be guided through a completely unfamiliar situation in the most intense environment cycling had to offer.

That set up the 1984 epic, with Fignon at the height of his powers – although no one suspected at the time that this was as good as it would get for him – and Hinault out for revenge. The tactical advantage lay with the younger man and his *directeur sportif*, who knew exactly how Hinault would race and could simply wait for him to tire himself out by attempting to put pressure on Fignon at every turn.

'It might have worked on a rider who was mentally weaker than me, but I never lost my head,' recalled Fignon.

'Guimard was smart,' says Robert Millar. 'He knew his riders, so during the '84 Tour he constantly poked Hinault's inner monkey so that he got angry and did something rash like attacking too far from the finish.

'As soon as Hinault heard the deedle-dee-deedle-dee of the Renault team-car horn he would start to tense up and then Guimard would appear in the bunch smiling and giving orders out to his team. The smiling part probably annoyed Hinault more than the orders.'

Guimard had other skills, recalled Fignon: 'When a break got a bit too far ahead, he was the only *directeur sportif* who would go up behind them with a stopwatch and work out their speed so he could tell us how fast the team had to ride. His calculations were usually 100 per cent reliable. Even with a nine-minute gap to a break, he could work out that if we began chasing at 62 kilometres to go, at a certain speed, we would bring them back three kilometres from the finish. It was impressive, and it played on the nerves of the other teams.'

Control freak Guimard might be, but he was level-headed enough to turn a blind eye when Fignon provided a blatantly shaky alibi for a team-mate who was supposed to be doing a press interview, but in fact had a rendezvous with 'an unofficial Miss France'.

Waiting in the wings at this point was Guimard's third great discovery, Greg LeMond, who had been 'scouted' for the Frenchman at the 1979 junior world championships. The story of how Guimard first saw him race is hilarious: he travels to the Ruban Granitier Breton, a race in Brittany, LeMond wins the stage, and within an hour of the start of the next day's stage he is in a break, three minutes up on the bunch, clearly heading for overall victory.

This worries Guimard, as he won't be the only one chasing his signature. Luckily for him, the American punctures and his team car is nowhere to be seen; when his *directeur sportif* eventually turns up,

LeMond throws his bike at the team car in disgust and quits the race. All the while, Guimard is in a car watching. His companion asks: 'Do you still want to speak him?'

'More than ever,' replies Guimard.

What he had wanted to see was a reaction of some kind: what he got was a *coup de gueule* worthy of Hinault.

As with Hinault, the plan hatched for LeMond was a long-term one after he signed with Renault in 1980, and, as with Hinault, Guimard was accommodating. Indeed, for a character who fell out so spectacularly with his protégés, Guimard would go to remarkable lengths to look after them.

When Greg LeMond arrived at Renault, the *directeur* not only hired Jonathan Boyer, a journeyman pro who happened to be the only American on the circuit, to nurse him in his early years, but Guimard also made the effort to learn English.

Similarly, he was surprisingly tolerant of LeMond's need for his wife Kathy to be at races on occasion, at a time when women were personae non grata for most teams and managers.

Guimard's divorce with LeMond – unlike with his other stars – was amicable, although he remained convinced that the American would have won more Tours had he remained at Renault rather than joining Hinault at La Vie Claire in 1985. LeMond recalled that when he left the French team, Guimard told him

he would win five Tours if he stayed, which does not
have a completely implausible ring to it: the American was good enough to take the 1985 race at least,
although whether Guimard's magic touch would have
saved him from the shooting accident that eliminated
him in 1987 and 1988 is pure conjecture.

The final radical move from Guimard came
in 1985. He had already changed the way French
cyclists at least earned their livings, by breaking
the monopoly held by Dousset and Piel, and when
Renault ended their sponsorship he and Fignon were
left high and dry.

Their answer was to change the way cycling teams
were run. Rather than the team being the property of
the sponsor, with the *directeur sportif* and the riders
as company employees, under the Guimard-Fignon
model the team was the property of a standalone
company – in their case Maxi-Sports Promotion –
which rented out the jersey space and publicity rights
for the riders to the sponsor.

In this case, the Système-U supermarket company paid the cash, 30 million francs, or about three
million pounds. An amusing footnote here was that
when Fignon and Guimard founded their company,
they chose a thrusting young Parisian lawyer as a
co-director. The future French president Nicolas
Sarkozy replied, when offered the role, 'Okay, but
don't ask me to do any work.'

The great strength of the system was that the

infrastructure of the team remained the property
of the holding company – in Fignon's words, 'A
marketing company whose role was to set up a cycling
team' – as the sponsors came and went. While many
other professional teams went down the Guimard
route in the late 1980s and through the 1990s, the
experiment of having the lead rider and the *directeur
sportif* as joint team owners remains unique –
imagine Bradley Wiggins or Mark Cavendish as
owners of Team Sky alongside Dave Brailsford –
and it was probably doomed to failure.

There was another issue which clearly caused
problems. Under the Guimard-Fignon system, the
profit for the directors of the holding company
consists of the difference between the sponsors'
subventions and the team's running costs. The
success of the venture depends on how the equation
is managed: the directors have to run a tight ship, but
in such a way that it is never prejudicial to the athletic
performance that brings in the sponsors' money and
earns the team rides in the major events. (There were
cases, in the 1990s, when I can recall riders turning
out for pro teams simply to make up the required
number of starters in a given race. I couldn't work
out how they had got in the team and could only
conclude they were extremely good value, i.e. riding
for nothing.) That's a hard balance to maintain.

Fignon, in his memoirs, states that he had
persistent issues with Guimard cutting costs. It is

impossible to verify whether this was the case, but in any case, the system meant there was room for the perception, it soured the relationship between him and his mentor, and that's all that matters.

The pair actually differed subtly over quite how to do it: Fignon wanted total independence from the sponsor, while Guimard wanted a closer relationship. A bone of contention between them was how much say the sponsor should have, for example in how the team raced. Currently, the signs are that Guimard had it right: in recent years some teams have begun reverting to something akin to the old model; Sky in particular are run the pre-Guimard way, with the team belonging to the sponsor.

The last flourish of greatness for Guimard's stable came during the 1989 Tour, but ironically enough what caught the public's imagination was Fignon's second place after his battle with LeMond. Both Fignon – in his memoirs – and his former *directeur sportif* rued the errors that they felt could well have lost them the Tour, most notably their blindness to the advantage LeMond gained by using his 'triathlon' handlebar extensions in the time trials, and their unwillingness to emulate him. Both state they had a strict principle that, in the Tour, only tried and tested kit should be used; even allowing for this, they should at least have appealed to the commissaires over LeMond's use of the bars, which were not within the rules.

There were opportunities that both could identify with hindsight when LeMond was vulnerable:
Guimard highlights the stage to Marseille when
Fignon had the American on the rack, but opted
to let Vincent Barteau win the stage rather than
attacking himself; Fignon pinpoints the stage to Alpe
d'Huez, when he was unable to attack LeMond on
the finish climb as early as Guimard wanted him to,
and the final Alpine stage to Aix-les-Bains, when he
escaped on a climb, but he and his DS agreed the risk
of a long-range assault was not worth taking.

As Fignon's career faded, the world Guimard had
built fizzled gradually away.

In 1991, Castorama fielded two leaders at the
Tour – Fignon, who had fallen out massively with
his former business partner, and Luc Leblanc, who
was being lined up as his replacement – and the two
men raced each other throughout the three weeks in
a venomous internecine battle which made Hinault
and LeMond in 1986 look like best buddies.

Fignon's star had faded, and his 'divorce' from
Guimard was a rancorous one; Leblanc would go
on to be a world champion for the now notorious
Festina team. After that came the ephemeral weird-
ness of Armand de las Cuevas, but Guimard's final
achievement of note at the Tour came in 1995, when
Jacky Durand took the yellow jersey in the prologue
time trial – a victory that owed more to freak weather
conditions than any of Napoleon's strategies.

In late 1996, one of Guimard's last acts as a
talent scout was when he took a 19-year-old Scot
named David Millar out for lunch with a view
to recruiting him for the Cofidis team, which was
being formed that winter. Guimard had lost none
of his skills at spotting future stars and winning
them over. It was, recalls Millar, classic Guimard: the
old magician still had his aura, still had the whole
Maxi-Sports set-up in Paris. Over lunch, Millar's
future for the next four years was mapped out, just as
Hinault's had been over two decades earlier.

'He had that Alex Ferguson quality,' recalls
Millar. 'You would go in as a junior and come out as
a champion. He was still the only guy in cycling with
a track record of nurturing guys from junior level to
Tour de France wins.'

While Guimard might be your first port of call
if you were a big-money French sponsor coming
into cycling, as Cofidis were, there was one issue: he
wasn't functioning in the same way that the rest of
cycling was. By the late 1990s, he was sadly out of
date. What had the biggest impact on a career by then
was not necessarily how a young cyclist was guided
and nurtured, not a four-year plan of campaign, but
could equally well be how his management interacted
with the doping culture.

'The golden age of *directeurs sportifs* who were
happy to carry out their work was over,' writes
Guimard in his memoirs. 'The time was gone when

we could set up strategies, make things happen in a race, when we were close to the riders, when we could build up a solid unit. We were no longer on the same planet. A *directeur sportif* could no longer live his passion to the full. What had become of his role as educator, of a talent scout? The doctors held the keys to success and had become the real bosses.'

The problem was that the world had moved on, in a way which was to be utterly self-defeating in the long-term for cycling. The prevalence of the doping culture at the highest level would mean a loss of the skills that had brought Guimard and fellow *directeurs sportifs* such as Peter Post and Giancarlo Ferretti their success.

The great team managers held the reins within their teams, the more so once they became willing to emulate Guimard and set up their teams as business-es in their own rights. If there is one thing Guimard should be remembered for, it is for the role he played in the sport's transformation from a rustic, amateur-ish model to something far more professional, led by the managers. Ultimately, however, that business-based model destroyed itself.

Ponder the lessons of the USADA report into the US Postal Service team, depicting as it does a world where recruitment for the lead echelon of the team is based on whether riders will blood-dope or not, where the race schedule is devised to suit the needs of the blood-doping programme, selection for the Tour is based on blood parameters, and where Michele Ferrari is available on the other end of the phone when Marco Pantani puts Lance Armstrong under pressure in the Alps at the Tour de France. Sport as Guimard forged it in the 1970s and 1980s had little place in that: biomechanics, psychology and career plans weren't the priority.

'I think part of Guimard's downfall was due to the fact that he did not embrace the doping culture,' says Millar. 'He was still very old school, but long-term planning and psychology no longer worked as they had done in the 70s and 80s. They had had a place until the early 90s, but everything Guimard had learned had gone out of the window.'

* * *

Guimard has had his personal struggles – most notably the collapse of the Ciclor company in 1996, which lost him his job at Cofidis – and has receded into the shadows. His retreat to the margins of French cycling was summed up when he received just seven votes in the campaign to be president of the French Cycling Federation in 2009.

He works with the Roubaix-Lille Métropole team and picks out the odd prospect – Andy Schleck being just one example – and is a popular media pundit, rarely off the airwaves thanks to his work for Radio Monte Carlo.

'He deserves a better place in cycling today than he is given,' says Madiot. 'A lot of people see only the wrong side of him.'

His legacy lives on in more substantial ways. Two riders who came through the Guimard mill as young talents, Jean-René Bernaudeau and Madiot, have built two of the most successful teams in France, with similar philosophies based on developing their own riders from a young age.

'All the guys who worked with him are marked by it,' says Quénet. 'They have all kept something of his, and are trying to reproduce what he did.'

'Of course I'm inspired by him, I could never say the opposite,' says Madiot. 'If I put emphasis on recruiting young riders, that's because I remember how he operated. There's a continuity there.'

Neither Madiot nor Bernaudeau has won the Tour yet, but who knows? The pendulum of power within cycling should be swinging back from the 'dodgy doctor' to the *directeur sportif*, and either may yet do so. And that would be true vindication for *Le Petit Chef*.

William Fotheringham has covered 23 of the first 99 editions of the Tour de France. His biography of Eddy Merckx, *Merckx: Half-Man Half Bike*, was the first cycling book to top *The Sunday Times* bestseller lists. A collection of his work at *The Guardian* since 1994, *Racing Hard*, has recently gone on sale, published by Faber and Faber. www.williamfotheringham.com Twitter @willfoth

9

Ellis Bacon gets interactive with a Channel 4 montage from the 1989 Tour de France, which is available to watch on YouTube.

The lead see-sawed between Frenchman Laurent Fignon and the USA's Greg LeMond before it was settled in the final time trial.

Channel 4's montage, compiled by 'tape genius' Jim Ramsey and set to a cracking soundtrack, captures the excitement of the greatest Tour of all and shows just how beautiful cycling can be.

THE GREATEST SHOW ON EARTH

BY ELLIS BACON

By 1989, I had what each of the leaders' jerseys meant pretty much sussed, including having got my head around the rules governing the multi-coloured 'combined' jersey, which I like to think was quite the cerebral leap forward in my development, aged just 12.

I'd watched my first Tour de France in 1986 – these days a haze of Greg LeMond-related yellow jerseys and an as-yet still unresolved conversation with my brother as to whether LeMond only had one lung, which, upon reflection, must actually be some kind of clouded recollection of his hunting accident that didn't actually happen until 1987, when the American suffered a collapsed lung, among other injuries, having been unintentionally shot by his brother-in-law.

Perhaps I'd had my eyes half shut in 1987 and 1988 – '87 with its nevertheless exciting 'It looks like Roche!' moment on La Plagne, and '88, which I thought was very forgettable, despite Pedro Delgado's positive-but-not-positive drugs test.

But, by 1989, I was on it, armed with a basic knowledge of team tactics gleaned from copies of *Winning* and *Cycling Weekly*, and a secondhand five-speed Eddy Merckx racing bike on which to test out my own racing prowess.

Watching Channel Four's coverage of the Tour was already a daily ritual – a half-hour programme Monday to Saturday, at 6.30pm, and then a full hour on Sundays, which you had to remember was on at 5pm or 5.30pm, or else miss it.

I would have said that we didn't have a video recorder then, but we must have just got one, as that year my brother and I recorded every stage, keeping them if they were good ones, and taping over them the next day if they were less exciting, knowing that the hour-long shows each Sunday – which we always kept, and still have somewhere – would provide a summary of the previous week's racing anyway.

On that final Sunday – the day of the Paris time trial at which, against all odds, LeMond overcame a 50-second deficit to win the Tour by just eight seconds from Fignon – we'd recorded the programme as usual, and I remember sitting down to watch it only on the Monday. No mainstream news coverage, no internet, no Twitter and no friends with even a passing interest in cycling meant zero chance of finding out what had happened before I'd had a chance to watch the tape.

But this isn't about that part of 1989 – it's about

the week that came before, beautifully, succinctly summed up by an extraordinary eight minutes of footage aired ahead of the final time trial, at the start of that Sunday programme.

I still have that videotape somewhere, but recently I discovered that the pre-stage montage had been uploaded to YouTube by 'MrPudsey'. Bravo to him for sharing with everyone what I knew already: that this nine-minute-and-38-second clip makes for the most stirring visual account of bike racing ever compiled.

Read on, and follow along with the time-codes on the YouTube clip, to be found here:

http://www.youtube.com/watch?v=VDznJwZvSKs

0:00 Those old, multicoloured Channel Four graphics fly onto the screen, the voiceover man introduces the programme, and then there's that familiar beat of the drums and the Andy Warhol-esque images that accompany the synth-pop of the Tour de France theme music. So familiar for so many years, it was the soundtrack to the oft-asked, unsolved question: 'Is that really Robert Millar in the polka-dot jersey, or simply a lookalike?'

As the Tron-like map of France fades away, along with the final note, it's straight into the Top Gun theme music of our first montage – with not a Tom Cruise, Kelly McGillis or Goose in sight. Instead, presenter Richard Keys informs us, 'We've come from Luxembourg…'

0:52 Cue guitar solo as Keys sums up the Tour so far. The script is spot-on; Keys has smashed it. But the best is yet to come as, resplendent in short-sleeved pink shirt and yellow tie, Keys introduces us to what will turn out to be an even greater summary of the final week of the race.

1:50 Violins herald the calm before the storm, as riders ready themselves for the off from a time-trial start-house...

2:28 A gentle trumpet – would a French horn not be more apt? – breaks us in gently, unknowing on first viewing the treat that lies ahead.

2:43 And there – yes! – a French horn, I believe!

3:01 Commentator Phil Liggett's voice cuts in, reminding us how Laurent Fignon lost his yellow jersey during the time trial on stage 15 between Gap and Orcières-Merlette. 'It's gone back,' he says. 'The pendulum swings again in the direction of the American Greg LeMond.'

3:19 In his awesome fluorescent pink Coors Light cap – which he appears to alternate with an equally desirable fluoro yellow one on other days – LeMond charmingly stumbles over his words: 'I don't feel there's probably any rar... rider riding better than me in the Tour de France...'

3:44 In the vein of the very best Westlife songs, we get a key change in the music, and now the pace is really on. A youthful-looking LeMond is introduced to the crowd by an even-younger-looking Daniel

Mangeas – still *le speaker* on the Tour today, his encyclopaedic knowledge of the riders and results no doubt even more honed now than they were then.

And just look at LeMond, in the days when the yellow jersey was provided by Castelli, which was then replaced by Nike, before a symbolic dropping of the American brand and a return to the Frenchness of Le Coq Sportif. Here, though, the jersey boasts an infinitely superior, simple black team logo rather than today's white sponsor panel.

And oh! How I wanted a pair of LeMond's sunglasses – Oakley Razor Blades. In the next shot, his baby-faced compatriot Andy Hampsten also has a pair and, as the two riders roll along, side-by-side, they're probably joking about how no one can afford their glasses.

4:00 'LeMond needs repairs', the caption informs us, but, perhaps even more importantly, and despite being clad in the yellow jersey, he's still using his normal, black team-issue shorts, rather than trying to match them to the maillot jaune. That would be a 1990s phenomenon.

4:42 Stage 17 to Alpe d'Huez sees Laurent Fignon go on the attack again.

'And there's Fignon having a go with four [kilometres] to go,' Liggett tells us.

'And Delgado has not reacted. Laurent Fignon lost a few seconds yesterday; he's going to take them back, and more, because Laurent Fignon has gone and Delgado… Who's worried about Delgado now? Because LeMond must react. LeMond could lose the yellow jersey here.'

5:03 And there, another 'want': LeMond's fluorescent yellow Avocet 30 bike computer, which I was lucky enough to get for my birthday, and which matched the fluorescent yellow Geoffrey Butler frame I later managed to save up for – a Reynolds 500 'training frame' – perfectly. To heck with LeMond's 'sagging' head, as Paul Sherwen describes it; I was dreaming of fluorescent yellow bikes and accessories.

5:31 'This race is not over, believe me,' LeMond smiles to the camera, in his pink hat again, 26 seconds down on Fignon overall at this point having lost the yellow jersey at the conclusion of stage 17.

5:46 The next day, France's other big hope, RMO's Charly Mottet, struggles, his legs and head lolling with the beat of the music.

For years afterwards, I'd tried in vain to identify the music track used, and YouTube poster MrPudsey – in the comments beneath the video – finally cracks it thanks to his mate 'Iain'. It's *Grand Designs*, by John Devereaux and David Reilly, which Jim Ramsey, who edited the montage, later confirms.

5:54 The beat continues in sync with a yellow-jersey-clad and attack-minded Laurent Fignon's pedalling.

6:11 For me, this is the really iconic moment of the whole montage: Delgado, LeMond and Dutchman Gert-Jan Theunisse, in the polka-dot jersey, fanned out across the road, almost in despair that Fignon has simply flown the coop. 'They've completely stopped racing. They've completely stopped racing,' Liggett repeats. The camera then appears to mimic him, rapidly zooming in-out, in-out, as the cameraman tries to focus as an exasperated Delgado ups the pace again.

6:32 The image of Fignon in full flight like this – hands comfortably on the drops, stretched out: a style that few have equalled, before or since – is how I like to remember him. Not the collapsed, despairing figure who lost the race by eight seconds three days later. Or the man who, as a 50 year old, lost all his power to the ravages of cancer. He died in 2010.

I was absolutely delighted, too, when, nine years after the 1989 Tour, while living in Avignon, in Provence, I decided to ride the 30 or so kilometres out to Uzès for the start of the now defunct one-day race, the Haribo Classic. Who should step out of the white car that pulled up just minutes before the start but Fignon... And then, following him from the back of the same car, LeMond! I had to pinch myself, watching these '89 foes, together, laughing and joking.

6:42 'And the crowd are standing up here, their hands above their heads. They applaud Laurent Fignon because he knows that today he's won the Tour de France – I'm sure of that,' Liggett says, emotionally describing the pictures of Fignon saluting the crowd as he wins the stage at Villard-de-Lans. LeMond is sixth, 24 seconds down, while Delgado follows, 33 seconds down on Fignon, in seventh place.

7:42 On stage 19, to the rumble of the drums in the soundtrack, LeMond opens his sprint to win ahead of Fignon in Aix-les-Bains, and the familiar French horn refrain comes back. LeMond would demonstrate that same straight-line speed again at the end of August when he won the world championships in Chambéry in a sprint from Russian Dimitri Kony-shev and Ireland's Sean Kelly.

Here, Fignon taps him on the back after the line, and LeMond does the same back. With Fignon now with a 50-second cushion, are both riders accepting that their overall places in the general classification are where they'll end up in Paris? LeMond certainly had other ideas…

7:56 They stand together on the podium – stage winner and yellow-jersey wearer – all smiles, just as I'd see them years later in Uzès.

8:09 First, though, there's stage 20 to get through. Usually, the final stage into Paris is the time for a demob-happy peloton to get up to a few high jinks – and for the winner to enjoy a glass of Champagne for the benefit of the camera. But in '89, of course, there was still a final stage to go after the 'fun' one.

Still, it didn't seem to stop anyone celebrating the end of the race. Fignon's Système-U team-mate, Vincent Barteau, was clearly that year's clown prince, hamming it up with a bit of the ol' 'shaky bike' and some choice faces for the camera. Barteau had won stage 13 from Montpellier to Marseille, on Bastille Day, no less, so could clearly be serious when he had to be.

The fun continues. Panasonic's Teun Van Vliet tries on Fignon's yellow jersey – and spectacles – for size, PDM's Marc Van Orsouw takes on Barteau at his own game, and Histor's Rik Van Slycke – today a sports director on Mark Cavendish's Omega Pharma-Quick Step squad – does his best Fabian Cancellara impression, more than two decades ahead of time, by hitching a ride on a motorbike. And we certainly wouldn't recommend PDM's Jörg Müller's 'trick' of stealing a police motorbike rider's revolver in this day and age…

Fignon, and his wife, close the montage: the former getting a whispered message from the latter – or 'Advice from her indoors' as the caption tells us. Brilliant.

9:23 'The sights and the sounds of the Tour de France,' Keys sums up as we return to the studio, 'brilliantly illustrated; Jim Ramsey the tape genius who's compiled those pieces for us.'

Jim Ramsey? I've heard the name each time I've watched the clip, of course – probably hundreds of times – and wondered who this man that beautifully captured 'the sights and the sounds of the Tour de France' was. Let's meet him…

BEHIND THE SCENES:
THE MAKING OF A MARVELLOUS MONTAGE

Jim Ramsey laughs when I remind him that Richard
Keys name-checks him at the end of the montage.

'I can never recall that happening before or
since,' Ramsey tells me from Riyadh, in Saudi Arabia,
where he's working on providing the country with a
more European style of football television coverage.
'Actually, saying that, it might have happened one
other time – in 1990, when I was just about to leave
London Weekend Television, and was working on
the football show *Saint and Greavsie*. I did a piece on
Cambridge United, who had kind of come out of
nowhere. Their manager – John Beck, I think it was
– would throw buckets of cold water over his players
when they came out onto the pitch before a game.
Can you believe it? We filmed it all. I think Dion
Dublin was playing for them at the time – before he
became a big name.

'Anyway, I went up there the day before with the
camera crew and, after two or three bottles of Barolo
with lunch, we blagged our way into all the university
colleges to get some footage. It was a four-minute
montage, but I think it was Saint [Ian St. John] who
pointed out that "there's one minute 28 seconds
before we see a football", because it was all about
the university.

'At the end of it, on air, Greavsie [Jimmy Greaves]

said, "Now, if you thought that was a bit arty, it's because Jim Ramsey did it. But he's leaving us next week, so don't worry – you won't have to put up with a piece like that again.""

Ramsey laughs again. 'He didn't put it nearly as nicely as Richard Keys did!'

Now aged 52, Ramsey says he has very fond memories of his time working on the Channel Four coverage of the Tour as a producer and director, and of 1989 in particular.

'I remember '89 very, very well, because it was an amazing Tour, with the lead changing hands so many times. And when it came to making those montages, I was allowed to do whatever I wanted; they never said to me they wanted a package at the beginning of the programme that was two minutes, or three minutes, or whatever. The fact that the longer one of the two was nearly eight minutes was because I felt that that was what it required. It was up to me to illustrate the skill, passion, endeavour, application, determination and camaraderie of the cyclists in a way that would appeal to television viewers.'

What he set out to do with it, Ramsey explains, was to combine music with bits of commentary – a bit like something he'd done before for the 1986 football World Cup.

'In 1989, the company I was working for to produce the Tour programme for Channel Four, TSL (Television Sport and Leisure), employed a lovely cameraman who I knew from my days at production company Cheerleader, who did American football for Channel Four, called Glenn Wilkinson. He changed it all: rather than just relying on the pictures from French broadcaster TF1, Glenn went out and shot race footage just for TSL and Channel Four, which meant we had a vast array of pictures to choose from.'

It was then a case of Ramsey logging every shot, and giving it a mark out of ten.

'So you might say, "Lovely scenic of," for example, "Bordeaux fields," and you'd give it a six, and then you might see an even better one with grapes in the foreground and cyclists going past' – as used in the first montage, in fact – 'and you'd mark it eight or nine. I still do it now.'

By the end of the week, Ramsey would have quite a collection, and could select the best images to use in the Sunday montages.

'On the Saturday night, we'd do the edit,' explains Ramsey, 'using all the best images from the week. I suppose it would take about four or five hours, until quite late at night. It's so anti-social working in sport!'

Another of the reasons that the final montage was so long, Ramsey says, is because he included more than a minute of the riders clowning around on the penultimate stage.

'One of the beauties of it for me was that Glenn

would get on very well with the riders. He had a tremendous rapport with them, and would get them to do silly things. Maybe 80 per cent of those pictures were his rather than French television ones.'

But the music, I venture, is equally as important as the images – at least, it would be hard to have one without the other.

'The track I used for the main part was a piece of library music…' Ramsey explains.

'*Grand Designs*, by John Devereaux and David Reilly,' I pipe up, quoting Iain and MrPudsey from YouTube.

'*Grand Designs*! Correct!' replies Ramsey.

I feel quite pleased with myself. I'd tried to find out what it was for years, imagining that I'd happily listen to that piece of music over and over on my Walkman, if only I could find out what it was.

'I'd listen to countless library-music tracks, so when I found that, I thought, "This is brilliant, this track,"' says Ramsey. 'I just thought that it sounded amazing, and seemed to suit the Tour well, as it wasn't 100 per cent 'pacey' music, and I wanted to mix it in with audio. But I was terrified of losing this one CD it was on, as I used it for a few other things, too, and for two or three years on the Tour – maybe more. It was certainly the best piece of library music I ever found.'

Demonstrating just how many times I've watched it, I ask Jim whether it was intentional that the music often kept pace with the riders' pumping legs, like with Charly Mottet at 5:46 on the YouTube clip.

'I wanted a piece of music that had pace, but also had some more emotional bits,' he says. 'Often, you get a piece of music that just has one tempo all the way through. Where I was lucky with that piece was that it had some different tempos that suited different moments.

'What you're not allowed to do, though, in theory, is edit the music, but what happens in reality is, underneath the commentary, nobody really notices when you edit it, so I did edit the music quite a bit,' he admits.

'But it's a very interesting, astute point you make about the rhythm,' he continues, and, for a moment, I swell with a pride that I feel has its roots in 1989, but has only now come to the fore. 'There were moments where I was waiting for a quicker bit of music for images like the ones you describe, and so I'd put in an extra scenic shot or extra image before it if the edit wasn't going to work.'

He also got a bit of stick for some of the captions, which he also wrote.

'That shot at the end of Fignon getting advice from his wife – "from her indoors" – for example!' he laughs. 'But it was in the days of *Minder*, so it was quite topical.'

Despite a seemingly faultless montage, Ramsey nevertheless has regrets about some aspects of it.

'I think what was a shame – I'll be honest – is that I left in the bit that Phil [Liggett] called wrongly on the day when Fignon went off on his own on stage 18, and those other three were left chasing.'

The bit he's referring to is at 6:49 on the You-Tube clip, when Liggett says, '… Because today he's won the Tour de France – I'm sure of that.'

'And of course he didn't,' Ramsey continues, 'although it did go out before the final time trial, so I didn't know what was going to happen.'

I reassure him that perhaps the montage is all the better for it, as everyone really did think that Fignon was going to win.

Liggett would have forgiven him anyway: the two men had worked together on the production of the Tour in 1985, and at the Seoul Olympics in '88.

'He asked me to be his agent,' Ramsey reveals, laughing. 'I was working at LWT at the time, and I said, "Look, Phil – I haven't really got time, even though I'd love to do it." He didn't earn that much with Channel Four in those days, but I stupidly turned down the opportunity and have been kicking myself ever since!'

At the 1985 Tour, British pro Paul Sherwen crashed on a descent near the start of stage ten, and chased the peloton for the rest of the day, for about six hours.

Surprisingly, he finished the stage, but, unsurprisingly, he was outside the allowed time limit, and so should have been eliminated from the race.

However, because of his dogged determination, the organisers decided to reinstate him.

'I suggested to Phil that we should do an interview with Paul, which we did,' remembers Ramsey. 'I'd already suggested that Phil should have a co-commentator – a suggestion he embraced. After the interview with Paul, I suggested that perhaps he might be the man for the job, and so Phil very kindly credits me with how his and Paul's double-act came into being.'

The pair now provide commentary for TV networks showing bike racing all over the world.

'I can honestly say that some of the most enjoyable moments of my life were spent working on the Tour de France for TSL,' Ramsey tells me. 'It was a great team, with Mike Murphy, one of my greatest friends, Brian Venner, Richard Keys and the lovely people at the Channel Four studio in Charlotte Street. I was given such a free rein by Mike and Brian to create something different for the start of the programme each Sunday.

'Perhaps the most important thing, in addition to the excellent feed of the host-broadcaster coverage from French television, was that TSL had invested in their own cameraman for the Tour, the enchanting Glenn Wilkinson, who provided those superb isolated pictures working with Steve Docherty in France. Glenn became the most famous British TV cycling cameraman, but then shockingly his life was cut short at the age of 44 in 2005. Mike Murphy had tragically died two years earlier, aged 51.

'The coverage in those years was innovative, thrilling and captivating,' says Ramsey, 'but, above all, it was Murph and Glenn who made it so fun and enjoyable, so all the credit should really be attributed to those brilliant, lovely men.'

Ellis Bacon is the former deputy editor of *Procycling*, and has written for a wealth of other cycling magazines and websites, including *Cycling Weekly*, *Cycle Sport*, *Cyclist* and *cyclingnews.com*, as well as for national newspapers including *The Times* and *The Observer*. He's covered nine Tours de France and, since going freelance in 2012, has written *World's Ultimate Cycling Races* (Collins) and translated controversial 1996 Tour de France winner Bjarne Riis's autobiography from Danish into English (*Stages of Light and Dark*, Vision Sports Publishing). His most recent book, celebrating the geography of 100 editions of the Tour de France, titled *Mapping Le Tour* (Collins), was published in May 2013.

10

Edward Pickering was in Paris in 2002 when all bar one of the living Tour de France champions took to the stage at the Palais des Congrès as the race prepared to celebrate its centenary.

He watched as they lined up next to each other and wondered whether they were extraordinary men or simply men who had achieved extraordinary feats.

THE TOUR WINNERS' CLUB

BY EDWARD PICKERING

The Tour winners' club is an exclusive, members-only society. It's unique, one of the smallest sporting fraternities in the world, and it has very French roots and customs, although it shares elements with two very different transatlantic institutions: the Masters golf tournament and the Presidency of the United States.

Like the Masters, its members have a dress code: a bright yellow jersey presented in Paris, a gaudy counterpoint to the conservative green jacket worn by the winner in Augusta.

The comparison with the presidency is more subtle. As with presidents of the United States, there is a hierarchy. Two-termers have a more exalted position than one-termers. And in the Tour winners' club, multiple winners trump single winners.

There's also a social pecking order, as there is in life, in which the more garrulous, or showy, or confident, or arrogant, or weird individuals rise to the top. Tour winners aren't just physically strong, their psychological armoury is formidable, too.

Eddy Merckx? He was the *Cannibal*! He crushed his rivals into the dirt! Bernard Hinault? The *Badger*! Pugnacious! Belligerent! He could start a fight in an empty room! Miguel Indurain was the strong silent type; Laurent Fignon prickly and oversensitive. Lance Armstrong? Well, he's been thrown out of the club now, but the list of flawed personality traits he exhibited was as big as the state of Texas.

At the presentation of the route for the 2003 Tour in the Palais des Congrès at Porte Maillot, just a couple of kilometres north-west along the Champs Élysées from the traditional finish line, the organisers celebrated the upcoming 100th anniversary of the race. All but one of the living winners were there to meet the public before attending an intimate dinner.

The Tour winners' club is mainly an abstract concept. There are no headquarters, no dimly-lit private room with soft music, discreet waiters and cigars, but on this one day in late 2002, the club was a real thing: the physical embodiment of 52 years of Tour-winning exploits all gathered together.

They lined up on the stage of the Palais des Congrès in front of an audience of peers, contemporary cycling stars, journalists, corporate guests, VIPs, fans, liggers and hangers-on: a line of men, upon whose faces were inscribed the effort, suffering and memories of cycling and life. They were introduced one by one, chronologically, but also ranked according to how many wins they'd achieved.

The single winners were up first: 1950 champion Ferdi Kubler, then, as he remains now, the oldest living Tour de France winner. Kubler was born in 1919, but he still moved with the optimistic robustness of his youth. He was followed on to the stage by the fragile, bent figure of Roger Walkowiak, and the overweight, bearded Charly Gaul. Each received a crescendo of applause that delayed and reverberated around the cavernous chamber, an echo of former glories. For just those few seconds, probably for the last time in their lives, each was once again the centre of the cycling universe.

Federico Bahamontes, still looking as skinny and energetic as when he won the Tour in 1959, Felice Gimondi, who looked like an aristocrat both on and off the bike, and Lucien Aimar, the jowly, grumpy organiser of the Tour of the Mediterranean, received their turns. Roger Pingeon, the 1967 winner, was the only absentee on the day, but he was still applauded. Jan Janssen, Lucien Van Impe and Joop Zoetemelk lined up, a short Belgian sandwiched by the two Dutchman to have won the race.

Then they presented Stephen Roche and Pedro Delgado, both men occupying the no-man's land between adulthood and middle age. Next: Bjarne Riis, Jan Ullrich and Marco Pantani, the three men who separated the Indurain era from the Armstrong era. The years fell away from the riders' faces as younger and younger men walked on to the stage. Ullrich and

Pantani were still professional cyclists at this point, their suits hanging more loosely around their bodies than their retired forebears.

Next came the double winners, and the applause grew louder. Bernard Thévenet, confident, and Laurent Fignon, shy, were welcomed on to the stage. A single triple winner: Greg LeMond, the blond hair replaced by grey, but the eyes as blue as ever. An unhappy quirk of circumstances meant that the next man on to the stage was then four-time winner Lance Armstrong, who by 2002 had fallen out with his American predecessor. Armstrong, tieless, chewed gum vigorously, and didn't look at LeMond. Nor LeMond at Armstrong.

Finally, the five-time winners emerged. Merckx walked onto the stage, and the applause was noticeably louder and longer than for all the others. The duration reminded me of stories of speeches by Josef Stalin, after which nobody wanted to be seen to be the first person to stop clapping, so they just carried on. The ovation was thunderous and prolonged.

Finally, Hinault – another very long burst of applause – and Indurain were presented. Hinault looks smaller in real life than he did as a cyclist, Indurain, taller.

And there they stood, 21 of the 22 living men to have won the Tour de France by 2002. The pantheon of the greats.

Gazing along the line of champions and ex-champions, it was impossible for a little of the adulation not to rub off on to me. I'd covered Armstrong, Ullrich and Pantani as a cycling journalist, and my feelings towards them were neutral. But others, further along the line to stage right, had been my boyhood heroes. Their faces used to gaze out at me from posters on my bedroom wall.

Even further down the line stood grey-haired men whose faces I could still recognise and transpose onto memories of seeing photographs of them in their racing days. Cycling's attachment to its past is more deep than other sports, and as a fan I considered the study of cycling's past essential for an understanding of its present.

I never saw Zoetemelk race, but he still wore the same vaguely haunted, unhappy expression he had when cycling. Van Impe had lost the bubble perm, but his face was unmistakeable even a quarter of a century after he won the Tour.

Of all of them, only Gaul was difficult to recognise, the best part of half a century living a hermit-like existence in Luxembourg having wiped almost all trace of his former life and achievements from his face and his frame. But the eyebrows, slightly raised, and the gap-toothed smile had survived across the years.

We feel like we know these people. They are special – in 2002, the living Tour winners' club numbered 22. Now, it is 25: Gaul, Fignon and

Pantani have died, while Armstrong was stripped of his wins. But Oscar Pereiro, Alberto Contador, Carlos Sastre, Andy Schleck, Cadel Evans and Bradley Wiggins have since earned membership. Compare that number to the couple of thousand people who have climbed Everest, or the 500 or so who have been into space. It is an elite group.

But are they special people? Or are they just ordinary people who have achieved special things? As a fan, I always thought it was the former. But the more I've interacted with the Tour winners, the more I've believed that there's a bit of truth in the latter.

The difference is perhaps that I grew up seeing these people win the Tour de France from a distance – I saw them on television, in magazines and newspapers and, occasionally, in the flesh as they flashed past me on the roadside. They appeared mythical, not real. Their coverage was sparse in English language media, which added to their mystery. I read books and magazines in French as a fan, to sate my need for more knowledge, and the accounts of their racing exploits, especially going back to the 1950s and 1960s, were epic and florid. They might just as well have been gods, or demi-gods.

But I've met most of them now. They laugh, are sad, get bored, get frustrated, work, divorce their wives, watch television and enjoy the company of their family and friends, the same as anybody.

They were gifted with the physical attributes of

a potential Tour winner, and harnessed the combination of work ethic and luck to allow the wear the yellow jersey in Paris.

The Tour de France is a competition of men, complete with assets and flaws – the confusion is that we mistake extraordinary achievements for extraordinary human beings.

In some cases, by making examples of these people, more harm than good is caused. Marco Pantani paid the ultimate price for his addiction to the adulation of the public. Lance Armstrong's uncompromising aggressiveness, cheered by whooping fans for seven consecutive Tours, now looks more sinister.

Show me a modern Tour de France winner, and I'll show you a complex character.

On the other hand, Bernard Hinault wouldn't have won five Tours without the stubbornness and strength of personality he had (they probably make him a nightmare to live with, but they are a real asset in a racing cyclist). Greg LeMond's sunshine-tinted optimism gave him three Tour wins – given the setbacks he suffered (child abuse, being shot in a hunting accident), if he'd had a pessimistic world-view, he'd never have made his comeback in 1989.

These are the famous examples. But what about the less well-known winners, the one or two-time Tour champions, from further back? I always felt like I knew Hinault, LeMond and the winners from the

careers coincided with
the sport. What are the

s of the two whose
ct on me, not for their
ordinary they seemed

ssential
m to
ssential

JAN JANSSEN — THE DOWN-TO-EARTH DUTCHMAN

Jan Janssen won his Tour in 1968. He was the first Dutchman to do so, and at the time, the 38-second margin of victory over Belgian Herman Van Springel was the tightest in Tour history. Janssen lived in Belgium at the time, and his win didn't go down well with the locals – they yelled abuse as he cycled past for years afterwards.

Janssen's Tour win was a masterpiece of patience, reslience and timing. He rode the chess player's perfect Tour, not even wearing the yellow jersey during the race, and taking it from Van Springel on the final stage time trial in Paris. His team-mates must have been happy about that – they rode for the winner, but never had to defend his lead.

The Dutchman was one of a cluster of riders who won the Tours in between the eras of Jacques Anquetil and Eddy Merckx, who each won five yellow jerseys.

As a one-time winner, he's less famous than those

riders, and could easily walk down the street without being recognised.

Of all the Tour winners I've met (some for hours, others for minutes), Janssen's the one who is least like a Tour champion. He's an ordinary man in a Tour winner's body – he was smoking like a chimney and getting scolded by his wife for it as we chatted over cups of tea, and later over *moules-frites* at his favourite local restaurant.

Janssen also struck me as extremely self-aware and thoughtful. There's no clear dividing line between historic Tour winners and 'modern' Tour winners, but I can't think of another winner since the early 1980s, at least, who would experience nostalgia for his past as Janssen did.

As we sat and talked, he showed me some old photographs and postcards of himself during his professional career, but lingered longest on one from the final time trial of the 1968 Tour. Lost in thought, he ran his fingers over his legs in the photograph, commented about how good the muscles looked, then just gazed at it for a while. When he started talking again, he told me about the power he felt on that day.

To be the best cyclist in the world is every competitive cyclist's dream. Days when cycling feels easy are few and far between, and he was lucky enough that one of his coincided with him being 16 seconds away from the yellow jersey on the final time trial of the Tour de France. (He actually started the 55-kilometre test in third place – noted non-time triallist Gregorio San Miguel of Spain was four seconds ahead of him.)

Janssen described the moment the fans by the roads started shouting '*maillot jaune*!' at him, at about halfway through, as being like a 'bomb going off'. He'd turned in that moment from a Tour contender into a Tour winner, and the confidence coursed through him. He must have felt omnipotent.

But the rest of the race hadn't been easy. When he described the ordeal of keeping himself in contention through the Pyrenees, Alps and Massif Central, he held his head in his hands and shook it, wincing. 'I suffered. How I suffered,' he said.

British cycling journalist Geoffrey Nicholson once described Janssen as one of the 'more forgettable' winners of the race, but what he really meant by that in modern terms would be 'less marketable'.

Janssen won his Tour (he also won Paris-Roubaix and the world championships – that winners' club has only six members, including Hinault, Merckx and Fausto Coppi) in an era when the event was important, but not internationally so.

Coverage and money was limited, so his exposure was limited. On one hand, it meant that he didn't live the life of fame and fortune that Merckx, LeMond and Armstrong experienced. On the other, it gave him the gift of an ordinary life.

BERNARD THÉVENET – THE FARMER'S SON

Fame changes people, they say. But Bernard Thévenet is an exception to this rule. He was born into the rural working class, in a *lieu-dit*, a settlement too small even to be classed as a village, called Le Guidon, in central France. In a twist on the concept of nominative determinism, where a person's name dictates their future job, '*guidon*' is the French word for a bicycle handlebar.

Thévenet won two Tours in the mid-1970s, and has become a respected and well-known television pundit in the subsequent years. But he's retained an air of humility and accessibility.

He also looks exactly the same as he did when he won the Tour – the skin on his face is a little more weathered and red-tinged, and there's a salting of grey hair among the thick black curls on his head, but otherwise, apart from the fact that he's lost the 1970s sideburns, he looks the same in his sixties as he did when he won his first Tour.

Where Jan Janssen is introspective and self-analytical, Thévenet is cheerful and open, which makes him as good a television pundit as his physical strength made him a cyclist. It also makes him an extremely good interviewee, and we sat in a café in Grenoble, his adopted home town, while he recalled his exploits with the practised ease of a raconteur.

Thévenet's a people person. Which makes it

interesting that the first Tour he won, in 1975, was less memorable to most people for the fact that he won than for the fact Eddy Merckx lost. That year was the Belgian's first defeat in the Tour de France – he'd won on his debut in 1969, and won every year since, apart from 1973, when he didn't start.

In contrast to Thévenet, Merckx is far less a social creature, which is probably a function of the fact that he's been public property in his home country since the late 1960s – 50 years of being asked for autographs probably makes one reluctant to strike up unnecessary conversation or offer pleasantries. It was also a function of Merckx's primary weapon: his ambition to win bike races.

Thévenet was the right man to beat Eddy Merckx – aptly for a race taking place in the French republic, the king of the Tour was being toppled by a member of the rural working class. Their contrast in characters gave their battle a human element, and made it easy for people to pick sides.

But something interesting took place when Thévenet won the Tour, over three days: he did change. On stage 14, to the Puy de Dôme, Thévenet's mindset was that of a losing contender. He'd put a bit of time into Merckx, who was suffering the effects of a crash, but like everybody else, he was basing his race around doing his best behind the Belgian. The next stage, to Pra Loup, was the day that made Thévenet famous – he chased down an audacious escape by Merckx, drew level with him on the final climb, then started squeezing out a lead. He was thinking and riding like a potential Tour winner.

But the transformation wasn't complete, even though the cycling public always fixated on this stage as Thévenet's moment of glory. In fact, it was less Thévenet's moment of glory as Merckx's moment of capitulation. The following day, Thévenet's journey from also-ran to winner to champion was complete – he launched a lone attack over the Col d'Izoard to win alone in Serre Chevalier, two minutes clear of second-placed Merckx. It was one thing catching Merckx on an off-day, another to thrash him and everybody else in another mountain stage.

But while his bearing and riding changed, Thévenet's roots in *la France profonde* were deep enough that they kept him anchored to who he was: an ordinary man in a Tour winner's body.

Edward Pickering is a freelance writer and former deputy editor of *Cycle Sport* magazine. He is the author of *The Race Against Time*, published recently by Random House, which covers the rivalry and careers of Chris Boardman and Graeme Obree. He also co-wrote three-time Tour de France green jersey winner Robbie McEwen's autobiography, *One Way Road*.

11

Rupert Guinness headed to the 1987 Tour as a wide-eyed rookie reporter intent on capturing the essence of the great French race.

His fellow Aussies may not have performed as well as he or his Australian editors would have hoped, but the duel between Ireland's Stephen Roche and Spain's Pedro Delgado ensured excitement all the way to Paris.

ROCHE AND THE ROOKIE REPORTER

BY RUPERT GUINNESS

It was January 1987, in the middle of a hot Australian summer, when the call came that would take me from the northern beaches of Sydney to the frost of an early European spring where a new road-cycling season had just begun with Switzerland's Erich Maechler winning Milan-San Remo.

The exchange was brief. Was I still willing to fly to Europe to take up the position of editor of the UK edition of *Winning* magazine?

The opportunity needed little sell. It was then *the* monthly cycling magazine, and for me it was my ticket to fulfilling my dream of covering the myriad one-day Classics and stage races I had only read about in *Winning*, including the biggest race of all, the Tour de France, which in 1987 was to start in West Berlin.

A few days later I was in England at the London Bike Show interviewing Frenchman Bernard Hinault, the five-time Tour winner who the year before had succeeded his throne to American Greg LeMond.

Sure, Maechler's Milan-San Remo win three days

earlier was still *le sujet du jour* for other journalists who
had interviewed Hinault earlier at the Look pedals
stand. But as a newcomer to the European scene, the
opportunity to talk about Le Tour with Hinault was
not to be missed. Neither of us knew then that more
than a quarter of a century later he would still be
referred to as the last French winner of the Tour.

At the time, I didn't know how long I would be
involved full-time in cycling, let alone the Tour. At
best, I thought my job at *Winning* would be the ideal
one-year 'working holiday' – a means to not just see
Europe, but to follow all the great bike races and get
a grasp of how they compared to the Tour.

I had no idea then that I would live in Europe
for nine years, even after leaving *Winning* magazine
18 months later: for four years in Belgium and five
in the south of France, working as US magazine
VeloNews's European correspondent and for a string
of other publications in the UK and Australia.

I would never have imagined that 27 years later,
now living back in Australia, I would still be covering
cycling and, *oui*, the Tour.

The 100th Tour, in 2013, will be my 25th as an
accredited journalist.

As an Australian, the highlight of those Tours
would have to be reporting on the first victory at the
Tour by an Australian – by Cadel Evans in 2011 – but
my first Tour in 1987 remains a standout.

It was a special year. The Tour winner, Irishman

Stephen Roche, became the first rider since Eddy Merckx in 1974 to claim cycling's 'Triple Crown'. He had won the Giro d'Italia earlier in the summer and then added the world championship road race in Villach, Austria.

Adding lustre to the impression of that first Tour for this wide-eyed rookie was that Roche had agreed that I write his daily Tour diary. Access to the top riders was easier then, in an era before the team buses arrived to limit it. During that Tour, I often wrote Roche's column after sitting down together on the sidewalk or at a café before a stage started.

Even better, the deal between Roche and *Winning* magazine required no manager, no contract, nor an exchange of money; a firm handshake sufficed.

That impression alone was ever-lasting. It is one that I have reflected on regularly in recent years on the Tour when I have been delayed before and after stages while waiting for riders to come out of the confines of the black-tinted-windowed buses for a few minutes to answer questions.

* * *

It still seems like yesterday when I first arrived in West Berlin on June 28, 1987, a few days before the start of the race.

On board a British Airways flight from Heathrow, England, with the British ANC-Halfords team on

board in readiness for its historic start, my first
glimpse of the Wall, which since its erection in 1961
separated East and West Berlin, was as we circled in
readiness for landing, was sinister.

I was not alone in temporarily allowing thoughts
of the Tour to be superseded by the history of the
Wall and the social and political divide it represented
between liberty in the West and the life of restriction
and virtual imprisonment by the communist East.

'Mate, that says something,' said ANC-Halfords
rider Shane Sutton – one of four Australians among
the 207 riders from 23 teams starting the Tour – as
he saw the Wall below us.

Sutton, the younger brother of world champion
track star Gary, was raised in the New South Wales
sheep-farming capital of Moree before he headed to
England to forge a successful career in racing. He did
not finish the Tour – the only time he started the race
– but 24 years later he would play an instrumental
role in guiding Briton Bradley Wiggins to his nation's
first Tour victory. No one would have seen that in
Sutton back then.

Sutton's remark about what he saw below was
not aimed at anyone in particular. For all I knew, he
could have been talking to himself. He would not
have known then that it was probably the last moment he would get to think of anything else but the
suffering of racing in the Tour for a while.

As I was an Australian journalist, Sutton's

presence on the Tour start list was important. Sure, he was not a star rider but, as a known raconteur, blessed with a dash of larrikin, a bit of a rogue, he could give an extremely good insider's read of a bike race, so I knew he would add value to my reports.

There were three other Australian riders in the 1987 Tour: Phil Anderson and Allan Peiper, of the powerful Dutch Panasonic team, and Czech-born, but only-recently-qualified Australian citizen, Omar Palov, who was on the ANC-Halfords squad.

All came with varying goals and ambitions. Anderson had finished in the top ten five times and worn the yellow jersey with distinction during two stints but, according to the European media at least, his career was coming to an end. Anderson suffered a back injury late in 1985 and had endured couple of seasons of flagging results.

Peiper was a seasoned *domestique de luxe,* whose dream had always been to help Anderson fulfill his potential. Peiper had ridden for Peugeot and now Panasonic with Anderson. Sutton and Palov were debutants and so they, like me, a rookie reporter, were finding their feet at the Tour.

Whatever dreams we'd had about the Tour came true when we landed in West Berlin. In the moment it took the West German customs official to stamp my passport and signal me to move on to collect my bags, conversation turned from the lack of civil liberty and freedom that existed behind the Wall to the Tour de France and who would do what, when, how and why.

Not that we were left without frequent reminders of what the Wall represented. Despite a first night spent in the cafés and bars that lined the wide boulevards of West Berlin, packed with so many accredited members of the Tour entourage who all seemed to know each other – a daunting scenario for this neophyte – the reality was that we were still several hours' drive away from the real free West.

All that connected us with Karlsruhe in the West was 'the corridor' through East Germany – an *autobahn* on which everyone would be warned several days later not to stop, no matter what the reason, or else risk being arrested.

And the reason we were in West Berlin was simple: to celebrate its 750th birthday. The city had paid the equivalent of $1.5million to host the Tour's *Grand Départ*: the presentation of the teams, the prologue time trial, the opening road stage, and then the stage two team time trial.

No matter how hard they tried – and succeeded – to provide the traditional pre-Tour excitement during the build-up, there was always an underlying sense that the 1987 Tour was also the subject of blatant politicisation.

And on no occasion was that politicisation more obvious than when the American 7-Eleven team were made to pose before Checkpoint Charlie with

US Marines, or against a backdrop of the Reichstag and the Brandenburg Gate where US President Ronald Reagan had visited 18 days earlier to address a massive West Berlin crowd in a bid to encourage – or force – the East to dismantle the Wall, as they eventually did in 1989, and to ready them for the forces of change and democracy.

Seeing East German guards in helmets and with rifles peering from shadowed outposts on the other side of the Wall at the building commotion caused by the 7-Eleven riders posing for the photographers, I quickly realised how the Tour was far more than a commercial sports event trying to globalise. It was also a platform for people to make their voice heard, and the West German council was willing to pay to hold it on their doorstep.

* * *

But there was far more to the 1987 Tour than the book-end of change it represents in my first-hand experience of it: it was a damn good race too.

Leading up to the Tour, many names were spoken of as likely contenders, but Roche emerged as the rider to watch after a string of top results during the spring and his aggressive racing style.

A fortnight or so before the Tour, Roche won the Giro d'Italia, while all of Italy rooted for his Carrera team-mate-turned-rival Roberto Visentini.

Roche's success carried extra weight as a pointer to his chances considering it had come after an off-season knee operation that could have ruined his career had it not been successful.

Albeit blinded by hope, faith or loyalty – or perhaps all three – I still hoped for a strong showing by Anderson. With the success of Australian cycling today, it is easy to forget the impact he made on the sport for the country during a professional career spanning from 1981 to 1994.

Anderson was the not the first Australian to race the Tour – 12 others got there before him – but he was nevertheless a modern-day pioneer for Australians. In 1981, he became the first Australian to claim the yellow jersey at a time when only a handful of English-speaking riders raced in Europe.

It was largely due to his efforts that today's riders enjoy such opportunity. His career pathway became a template for others to follow.

After racing for the Paris-based amateur Athletic Club de Boulogne-Billancourt (ACBB) cycling team, and having joined the French professional Peugeot squad, his progression was rapid as he led a new wave of English-speaking riders, which included Peiper and Roche – both former 'ACBB-ists' – who also went on to join Peugeot and become known collectively as 'the Foreign Legion'.

Anderson's career became a benchmark of excellence for so many in Australia after he first beat

Hinault to take the yellow jersey on Pla d'Adet at the 1981 Tour, eventually finishing tenth overall, before returning in 1982 to wear the *maillot jaune* for nine days, winning a stage along the way, and then taking fifth place overall in Paris. At the 1983, 1984 and 1985 Tours, Anderson placed ninth, tenth and fifth, respectively, before a chronic back issue – sacroiliitis – in late 1985 put his career in jeopardy.

Anderson had joined Panasonic, the powerful Dutch team, in 1984 and renewed his contract after his fifth place at the 1985 Tour. But the hereditary rheumatic back ailment flared up and cost him the world number one ranking at the end of that year and forced him to miss half of the 1986 season. He returned to finish 39th in that summer's Tour as part of a carefully-planned comeback.

But Peter Post, his sports director at Panasonic, a hard, uncompromising Dutchman, was nevertheless running out of faith in Anderson.

Where once Post had been glowing in his assessment of Anderson, he capriciously and publicly changed his mind, although he did still select him for the 1987 Tour. Rightly or wrongly, Post's word was treated as gospel within cycling and his criticism of Anderson had a double-edge to it.

Perhaps he thought it would inspire Anderson to prove him wrong but it also watered down the rider's previously high value on the market.

Many European journalists sang from Post's

hymn sheet and so any time I suggested that Anderson might be on the verge of returning to his best form was met with an array of winces, frowns and shakes of the head.

Thinking of the freelance work I'd committed to in Australia, I began to wonder if I'd missed the boat. Maybe Anderson's best days were behind him and perhaps there would be little of interest to the Australian readership at this Tour.

* * *

Fortunately, my primary responsibility at the 1987 Tour was to write for *Winning*'s special weekly issues, meaning that an Australian angle was not essential. But I wanted to convey the scale of the Tour to an Australian audience in my columns for the now defunct *Sun News-Pictorial* – a Melbourne daily tabloid that has since morphed into the *Herald Sun*.

So I was delighted to discover that the first rider to tackle the 6.1-kilometre prologue time trial on an inner-city circuit through West Berlin's Kurfürstendamm would be Shane Sutton.

Although his time was bettered by all but five riders, it could not alter the fact that, for a few minutes, and perhaps not in the most conventional sense, an Australian had led the Tour de France.

Anderson failed to silence his doubters. He was the best Australian in the prologue but was only 63rd, well down on the flying Dutchman Jelle Nijdam, who covered the course in seven minutes and six seconds to take the first yellow jersey of the race.

Roche, meanwhile, dispelled any concerns that he would be tired after winning the Giro by finishing third behind Nijdam, who was a specialist at these kind of short, sharp solo efforts.

'I was surprised,' Roche said in his first diary entry. 'I didn't think I would have beaten a lot of the riders who should have been up there. At the start I did go out very quickly, but then I felt the legs went a bit flat. I couldn't use the big gears.'

Over the next few days, Roche enjoyed a trouble-free spell. He stayed in third place, 19 seconds behind the Pole Lech Piasecki, after stage two, the 40.5-kilometre team time trial in West Berlin.

But he was worried about his Carrera team-mate Urs Zimmermann, the Swiss rider who was third overall in the 1986 Tour and had been earmarked for a vital support role in the mountains. Zimmermann, impeded by a nagging injury to his backside after a crash at the Giro, rode at the back in the team time trial and looked out of sorts.

Then came the 750-kilometre transfer from West Berlin to Karlsruhe, which required running the gauntlet of 'the corridor'. The East German border guards were keen to allow a smooth passage in exchange for Tour souvenirs.

When the racing resumed, another of Roche's

Swiss team-mates, Erich Maechler, took the yellow jersey after finishing second behind Portugal's Acacio Da Silva on the 219-kilometre third stage from Karlsruhe to Stuttgart.

Maechler held the yellow jersey for six days, which, as time wore on, began to concern Roche. He was not keen about his team investing so much energy defending the lead when Maechler had no chance of winning the Tour outright.

'I always thought it would be a risk,' Roche said; 'The defence was made, though, and people will be looking for us to make a move. The pressure is now on us, which is not what I wanted.'

Roche's concern was valid. To assume control so early on risked exhausting his riders physically and mentally before they reached the crucial final week. While other teams saved energy riding within themselves, the team with the yellow jersey chased down dangerous attacks, some of which may have been launched purely to force Carrera to react so they would get tired.

In Troyes, at the end of stage seven, the Carrera team had more cause to celebrate – although the joy was to be short-lived – when Guido Bontempi won the sprint.

After the eighth stage to Epinay-sous-Sénart, Roche declared enough was enough. He was happy to know that Maechler would lose the lead in the time trial so Carrera could afford to loosen the reins during the flat stage which preceded it. 'The plan is to keep the yellow jersey until tomorrow. [Charly] Mottet should take it for Système-U before or during the stage ten time trial,' he said.

While Mottet did indeed take the yellow jersey from Maechler, it was Roche who shone in the 87.5-kilometre time trial from Saumur to Futuroscope. By winning the stage – 42 seconds clear of Mottet – he moved into sixth place overall and established himself as a potential Tour winner.

'I knew I was on a good ride, but not a winning ride because I couldn't get time checks on Charly Mottet as he started after me,' Roche said.

Although Roche had climbed up the overall standings, he was still three minutes and 23 seconds behind Mottet, who was a good climber.

Roche was coy – or uncertain – about when he would launch his first strike for the race lead. All the Irishman would – or could – say when asked was: 'I will just follow and watch the groups don't get away with people like Laurent Fignon. I might just see how Mottet goes – see how he goes under pressure.'

Anderson, meanwhile, was forlorn. The night before the time trial he said it was an opportunity for him to prove Post wrong.

'The team hasn't got a lot of confidence in me at the moment. The time trial is very important for that. I will be looking for a good time there.'

He failed. According to one Belgian journalist,

Post – never the most diplomatic or sensitive individual – said that Anderson rode like a 'retarded human being' to finish ten minutes behind Roche, dropping from 56th to 61st place overall.

Anderson was shattered.

'I just didn't have it. I don't know what happened. I guess you could say it was the worst time trial I have ever done. I am as fit as I have ever been and my training has been good. I am just not getting the results I need,' Anderson said before cycling from the stage finish to begin wrestling with his fate on the cycling world's biggest stage.

For Roche, the more the peloton settled into some sort of order, the more comfortable he felt.

Mottet lost the yellow jersey to his team-mate Martial Gayant, who won stage 11 at Chaumeil, by which time the Pyrenees were on the horizon.

'I am coming around now. I am pretty happy. I am hoping, in the mountains, it will be a process of elimination,' Roche said. 'I will move up as people drop back. Then I won't have to attack.'

The Dubliner even went as far as to accept the mantle as the latest Tour favourite.

'I suppose I am the favourite, but we all like to say each other is the number one. That puts the pressure on them. Mottet will say I am, I will say he is – it works that way.'

No doubt about it: Roche was playing mind games. With the mountains looming, he wanted as little pressure on him as possible, and so he welcomed the ease of pace at the start of the 228-kilometre 12th stage from Brive-la-Gaillarde to Bordeaux.

The big story for the small band of reporters who were writing for US publications was the sprint victory by Davis Phinney in Bordeaux but for everyone else the story of the day was the crash that put Irish hard egg Sean Kelly out of the race.

The image of a tough-as-teak Kelly in tears, with his head on the shoulder of his Kas team's sports director Christian Rumeau when he stopped riding 20 kilometres after sustaining a suspected broken collarbone in a crash, is as vivid now as then.

Another memory was the arrest that night of two suspected Basque terrorists for allegedly planning to attack the Tour on July 14 – Bastille Day – when the race was to pass the French-Spanish border. It was another incident that reminded me of the social impact that the Tour can have on Europe.

Anticipation was high for the first day in the Pyrenees, the 220-kilometre 13th stage from Bayonne to Pau, but while there was no Basque intervention as feared, it did introduce the 25-year-old Frenchman Jean-François Bernard as a man to watch.

Bernard did not win the stage – he was second to Dutchman Erik Breukink – but, significantly, he rose to second place overall behind Mottet, who took back the yellow jersey from Gayant.

The French had Mottet in the lead and Bernard

poised a minute and 52 seconds back in second place, resuscitating hopes of a home winner.

Roche was not too concerned by Mottet because he could be brittle in the high mountains but, while the Irishman sat happy in third place, he was looking over his shoulder at Spaniard Pedro Delgado, who had risen to sixth place.

For the favourites, the race had entered its critical phase. The Pyrenees represented a metaphorical turning point and that had been no more clearly highlighted than by the sight of Sutton, straddled over his bike, his head hung low and elbows leaning on the handlebars, well before the start of that stage from Bayonne to Pau.

The bell rang, telling the riders that there were 20 minutes to go until the start, but Sutton was already on the sun-baked start line, alone.

Other riders were enjoying a coffee in a shaded café or sitting in their team cars, calming their nerves for the first mountain stage.

But Sutton, the last man in the overall standings, wanted to get the torture that awaited him over and done with. The agonising climbing that awaited in the sinewy, steep and lumpy roads that led to the summits of the Pyrenean mountains worried everyone but Sutton was not thinking of how many mountains were ahead; just the first one. He would deal with them one after the other – or so was the plan.

The answer was there before Sutton even started.

After approaching to say 'G'day' with a soft pat on his shoulders, he looked up at me and managed a smile. But the hollow eyes and gaunt face showed he was on the brink of exhaustion. I sensed that making it over the first mountain might be too much to ask.

Little wonder, then, that the rider who for a few minutes in West Berlin, had led Tour, found himself pulling out, 70 kilometres before the first major mountain of the race. Just like that, Sutton's first and only Tour de France was over, and it was probably for the best.

* * *

For Roche, the Pyrenees signalled the start of the real battle. The 166-kilometre 14th stage from Pau to the summit of Luz Ardiden was won by a solo attack from 7-Eleven's Dag-Otto Lauritzen. The former Norwegian policeman started cycling as part of his recovering from a knee injury sustained in a parachuting accident.

While Lauritzen was little threat overall, Roche was nevertheless agitated by the tactics of rival teams. He had become frustrated by the way the front part of the peloton would split between the climbs but always regroup towards the summit. No one was assuming the responsibility of pressing the pace on the climbs and, although he had narrowed Mottet's lead to a manageable one minute and 26 seconds, he was worried by the way the favourites were bunching together at the top of the general classification.

'There is no real tactical battle. It is getting frustrating. There needs to be a team strong enough to dominate the race. There isn't, though.'

The mounting tension showed the next day on the 164-kilometre 15th stage from Tarbes to Blagnac that was supposed to have been a quiet day for Roche. The stage appeared set to remain calm, even after a break escaped and stayed away to the finish, where German Rolf Gölz won.

But in the German's wake, the peloton split in two, partly because of a torrential rainstorm, and Roche surprisingly found himself badly positioned and caught in the second group, losing valuable and hard-fought time. Understandably, he was angry to slip back and find himself two minutes and 33 seconds down on Mottet and frustrated at his team's inability to help close the gap after the split.

'We were all one group and all of a sudden a big gap opened up. Before we knew it, we were 400 metres behind. A lot of my guys were mucking around at the back,' Roche said.

'Yesterday, most of them finished around half an hour down, so there was no excuse to have sore legs. What upsets me so much is that I worked so darn hard yesterday to gain time on Luis Herrera [now eighth overall at eight minutes and 34 seconds], and then I lose it so stupidly.'

Roche's doggedness did not weaken. He cut his deficit to one minute and 26 seconds on the 16th stage from Blagnac to Millau, won by Frenchman Régis Clère, by which time the talking point was the brewing battle for the yellow jersey between Roche, Delgado, Bernard, American Andy Hampsten and Mexican Raul Alcala.

Roche's fourth place on the stage soothed his frustration at having lost time to Mottet at Blagnac: 'I was happy that when the crunch came I was able to go with them.'

He also said while he was not as exhausted at the summit finish as he had been at Luz Ardiden, he bluffed to cover his pain on the last climb.

'For Hampsten, Delgado and all that, I am their strongest rival. I have to show them I am not weak, that I am strong. I can't let them know when I am feeling weak.'

It was then, with Delgado fourth overall at three minutes and 16 seconds, that Roche began to talk of the race lead.

'There is no point in taking it now. We just have not got the team to defend it that long,' Roche said. 'When I take it I don't want to let it pass back to some-one but I've been thinking about the right time.'

The next two days gave Roche that time to think, but then – following a rest day – came one of the most crucial stages. Stage 18 was a 36-kilometre time trial from Carpentras to the 1,912-metre summit of

Mont Ventoux – a gruelling climb that is part of cycling folklore, and admittedly of a stature that, in 1987, I probably didn't appreciate in its fullest until after the stage.

No mountain on the race is more feared by riders and loved by fans than Mont Ventoux where, at the 1967 Tour, British cyclist Tom Simpson died despite efforts to revive him after he collapsed on the barren scree slopes nearing the top.

Still, it wasn't until 1987, as I sat near the memorial plaque that has been placed in honour of Simpson and watched the riders pass one by one, that I really appreciated how torturous the climb is with its average 7.8 per cent gradient, as well as the added physical and mental stresses from the wind and suffocating heat and humidity.

Roche tipped the French revelation, Bernard, as a potential stage winner.

Bernard lived up to the expectation, winning the stage and the yellow jersey. Colombian Luis Herrera was second, with Delgado third. Mont Ventoux always favoured the naturally gifted climbers. Roche, more of a fighter than a *grimpeur,* was fifth, conceding two minutes and 19 seconds to Bernard, who had leapfrogged him overall.

Bernard was now considered a major threat; Mottet, having slipped from first to third, less so. Delgado, who was fourth, was now beginning to look very dangerous.

Roche lamented he 'would have preferred to have gone faster at the start, but I was afraid of blowing up', and said that he expected an aggressive final week. He also knew that whatever reserves he still had would be needed in the Alps.

'From now on, I will attack. I feel fresh and I feel less tired than I usually do after a time trial. I have noticed Bernard is always less tired than us on the last climb,' he said, 'so perhaps I will have to attack early in the race and surprise him.'

It was ironic that, the day after Mont Ventoux, the 1987 Tour reported its first positive test in an anti-doping control since Simpson's death, when amphetamines and alcohol were found in his system.

There had been other doping scandals on the Tour – such as that of Belgian Michel Pollentier who was booted from the race for attempting to cheat a dope control in 1978 – but, until 1987, no positive test had been confirmed.

Even worse, for Roche's Carrera team, one of the two riders caught was Guido Bontempi, who was stripped of his stage win at Troyes. The German Didi Thurau was the other rider.

In light of the understanding of recent events, it may sound bizarre to read that little was made of the scandal. In an age of naivety and blind innocence that lasted far too long, I remember being warned against talking too openly about it because some Fleet Street journalists from England were due to pop across the Channel to cover the Tour now that Roche was edging closer to a win.

No one wanted the positive tests to become much more than a footnote. It's little wonder the problem of *omertà* prevailed and extended so far.

Roche was concentrating on the race and his read on the tactics was dead on. So sharp were his predictions, it was like he had a crystal ball.

As impressive as Bernard's win at Mont Ventoux had been, the hopes of a French winner were short-lived. Bernard's single day in yellow ended in disaster. It was the 185-kilometre 19th stage from Valréas to Villard-de-Lans – the first day in the Alps. Bernard punctured on an early climb and was later attacked by Système-U and was left without team-mates to a lonely chase.

For the first time, Delgado and Roche emerged as the two men most likely to fight for the Tour. The Spaniard won the stage and Roche took the yellow jersey. The battle lines for a thrilling head-to-head were drawn.

'It is the first time I have worn the yellow jersey in the Tour. I have long waited for it. It would be the greatest day of my life to keep it,' Roche said

The Irishman still knew that as quickly as he claimed the race lead, he could lose it, especially to Delgado who was now third overall.

As Roche said: 'The Tour is not over yet. I may not even have the jersey after tomorrow.'

Again, Roche's read of the race rang true. Delgado took the yellow jersey from him at Alpe d'Huez, after the 20th stage, won by Spaniard Federico Echave.

Delgado had taken a considerable amount of time out of Roche, who fell to second overall, 25 seconds behind the Spaniard.

Just as it had been for Roche the day before, claiming cycling's most prestigious jersey at Alpe d'Huez was an emotional achievement for Delgado. The previous year, while fifth overall, Delgado had abandoned the Tour on the way to Alpe d'Huez after being informed of his mother's death.

By taking the yellow jersey Delgado became the first Spaniard in 14 years to do so – the last having been Luis Ocaña. But he was still a long way from making the yellow jersey his own for good. Opportunity awaited Roche in the next two mountain stages, and in the time trial at Dijon on the penultimate day.

The drama of Roche's finish at La Plagne still remains one of the most spectacular finales in a mountain-top finish I have ever seen.

Frenchman Laurent Fignon won the stage from his Spanish breakaway companion Anselmo Fuerte, whose beating of his handlebars as he took second placed reinforced how hard the pair had raced for the day's honours. But that still did not match the intensity of the Roche-Delgado duel behind them. Both Tour contenders tipped all they had from the toy box to get the upper hand.

Delgado attacked Roche, knowing, with the time trial to come, he needed a bigger lead to win the Tour. Hitting the last climb, the charismatic Spaniard had 90 seconds or so on Roche. And that gap remained constant until the last five kilometres, where Roche began to peg back time on Delgado.

Delgado was defiant to the end, taking fourth place on the stage 57 seconds behind Fignon. But Roche was fifth, only four seconds further back after digging so deep into his reserves he collapsed just after the finish line where he received the assistance of his mechanic and friend Patrick Valcke, and was then given oxygen by the Tour's medical staff for 15 minutes before being taken to hospital by ambulance for observation.

Roche was soon back at his hotel, 29 seconds down overall on Delgado and with little more to say than: 'I have to make sure I recover properly and an early night is the best remedy.'

He told Irish TV: 'I couldn't breathe, I couldn't get off my bike, I couldn't stand. I was lying on the road and across the finish was a big scaffolding and all the journalists were up there getting photographs. It was swaying and creeping. I thought: "That's going to come down on top of me." I couldn't do anything about it. I was in a daze, then they gave me the oxygen. It helped me breathe better, and I came round.'

Did he ever. The next day, the 22nd stage from La Plagne to Morzine, Roche rode brilliantly, as did his loyal *domestique*, the Belgian Eddy Schepers, who remained by his side all the way up the final climb, the Col de Joux Plane.

The tactic by Schepers was to ride at a tempo that Roche could follow, but that would also deter his rivals from attacking.

Spaniard Eduardo Chozas got away to win the stage, but over the Col de Joux Plane Roche dropped Delgado, took second place and cut back his overall deficit to Delgado to just 21 seconds.

'It was my last chance to make up time on Delgado before the time trial at Dijon,' Roche said. 'It is going to be a head-to-head battle. I am not saying I have won the Tour yet. It is not over until Sunday night. But today has put it in my favour.'

When it came to the final time trial, the day's honours went to Bernard. But as late afternoon rain began to fall, making the 38-kilometre course damp and dangerous, Roche, who took the corners cautiously to avoid crashing, finished second at one minute and 44 seconds. More importantly, Roche had beaten Delgado by one minute and one second. That was enough to put the Dubliner first overall, 40 seconds ahead of Delgado – an outcome that initially aroused relief more than joy from Roche.

Not that Roche held his joy in for long.

On the last day, stage 25 from Créteil to the Champs-Élysées in Paris, there was plenty of Irish 'craic' on the roadside.

It wasn't all about the Irish. American Jeff Pierce of the 7-Eleven team won the stage. Anderson, my *raison d'etre* for being on the Tour in the first place, dug deep to take a creditable tenth place on the stage.

But it was Roche's day – and deservedly so after such a dogged scrap with Delgado for the Tour title. Amid the celebration and back-slapping, he reminded people: 'I never said I would win; people said it for me. I always thought about it, but I never believed it. When you actually cross the line knowing you've won, you don't feel really different.'

But he did admit that 'when they play the national anthem and you see Irish people in the crowd, it is very touching'.

That was evident as Roche stood on the Tour podium while *The Soldier's Song*, the national anthem of Ireland was played. Tears welled in his dark, beaming, smiling Irish eyes. How much better could it get? At the time, it didn't even matter. For Roche. For Ireland. For the Tour.

I was thrilled to have finally reported on an event that I had always wanted to cover; even better that I got to write the eventual winner's diary.

But no one – no one I knew – forecast that several weeks later Roche would be back on the podium celebrating victory in the professional road race world championships in Villach, Austria.

It was a win that meant he became only the second person – Eddy Merckx being the first – to claim the Giro d'Italia, Tour de France and world championship titles in the same year.

As for Anderson and the other Australians, there was little success to celebrate at the 1987 Tour. Only Anderson and Palov finished, 27th and 103rd overall, respectively, while Peiper and Sutton made early returns home.

But their performances did little to deter me returning to the race year-in, year-out. They may not have won, but they inspired.

And in time – albeit plenty of it – Australians were to truly shine at the race. There were spells in the yellow and green jerseys for the likes of Stuart O'Grady and Robbie McEwen, Baden Cooke and Brad McGee. There were stages wins by McEwen and Cooke, and, finally, a first Australian Tour title, for Cadel Evans in 2011.

For me, the long wait, and my appreciation of the long, steady journey to ultimate success, was made all the richer by my experiences in 1987.

Rupert Guinness is the cycling writer for the *Sydney Morning Herald* (Fairfax) and a former editor of *Winning Bicycle Racing Illustrated*, European correspondent for *VeloNews* and contributor to *The European*, *Cycling Weekly*, and *Cycle Sport*. He has been covering cycling since 1986 and the 100th Tour de France will be his 25th. He has authored 13 books, the most recent two being *The Tour – Behind the Scenes of Cadel Evans' Tour de France* (Hardie Grant, 2012) and *We Won't Back Down – On the Road with Orica-GreenEDGE* (Allen & Unwin 2013). He now lives in Sydney.

12

The Festina Affair in 1998 did not spell the end of cycling's relationship with performance-enhancing drugs.

Successive scandals and the fall of Lance Armstrong have made this seem like the dirtiest era the sport has ever known. The Tour has ridden through storm after storm in the past 15 years.

Lionel Birnie marvels at the race's powers of recovery and realises it is, surely, the most resilient sporting event of all.

A GUIDE FOR THE CYNICS AND SCEPTICS

BY LIONEL BIRNIE

On Wednesday, July 8, 1998, two unrelated events happened at roughly the same time. At about 7.45am, an envelope fell through my letterbox containing a contract confirming I was to start work as a sub-editor at *Cycling Weekly* in August.

Meanwhile, at about quarter to seven French time, Willy Voet was driving a Festina team car across the border that divides Belgium and France. As he explained in his memoir, *Massacre à la chaîne*, Voet had decided at the last moment to pull off the motorway and cross the border on a back road. The significance of that change of direction was huge.

Voet was driving down Rue du Dronckaert when he saw the customs officer signalling at him to pull over. 'Dronckaert' means 'alcoholic' in Flemish but he wasn't concerned about being done for drink-driving. In the boot of his car were 234 doses of EPO, which stimulates the production of red blood cells, which in turn helps transfer oxygen around the body more efficiently – something vitally important to endurance athletes. There was also human growth

hormone, testosterone and blood-thinning drugs so
riders could bring their haematocrit levels below the
50 per cent limit imposed by the sport's governing
body, the Union Cycliste Internationale (UCI).

Voet, who worked as a *soigneur* for the Festina
team was taking the drugs to the Tour de France,
which was due to start in Dublin at the weekend.
They were intended for the Festina riders, including Richard Virenque and Alex Zülle, two of the
favourites to win the race, and Laurent Brochard, the
world champion.

It took a day or so for the news to reach Ireland,
where it cast a shadow over Dublin's *Grand Départ*,
organised, in part, by Pat McQuaid – now president
of the UCI. The denials were swift, as they always
are, and the show went on, as it always does.

But what began as a distant rumble soon became
a seismic event. The shockwaves rattled the rafters
and shook the foundations, and by the time the race
was back in France, the whole house nearly crumbled
to the ground. As with some earthquakes, it can be
the aftershocks that cause the most damage.

For three weeks that summer, the Tour was
engulfed in the flames of scandal, and I reacted like
any fan. I tried to play down the significance of the
arrests and I fell for the line that this was a case of a
few bad apples.

'I could take drugs but I still wouldn't be able to
ride over the Alps the way they can,' I said. This was

true, but it also missed the point by a country mile.

'If the riders were allowed to take whatever they wanted, it would be a level playing field.' I hadn't yet realised that would mean all competitors would be compelled to cheat and take risks with their health, such was the potent effect of the combination of drugs the cyclists were taking. Nor did I realise that people respond differently to those drugs, particularly EPO. After taking the same dose of EPO, there was no guarantee that two riders of similar natural ability would remain evenly-matched. That is where the doctors came in. It wouldn't be a level playing field, it would be sport created in a syringe. I hadn't yet processed all this. I didn't know enough.

* * *

I knew there was a history of drug-taking in cycling. The stories of doping added a Machiavellian streak to the Tour's history. I knew the story of Tom Simpson's death on Mont Ventoux and how amphetamines and alcohol had been found in his bloodstream during the post-mortem. On a family holiday to Provence as a teenager, we'd made a day-trip to see his memorial. I looked at the road and imagined him weaving and wobbling. I picked up a stone from the rocky scree and put it in my pocket. I remember feeling how warm the top side of the stone, exposed to the summer sun, felt compared to the cool, clammy underneath. And I was left with one thought. Was the Tour de France worth dying for?

After Simpson's death, attitudes changed, outwardly at least. Doping had been banned in the mid-60s and anti-doping tests were carried out at the Tour for the first time in 1966, but the death of a rider struck at the heart of the Tour. The 1968 race was dubbed *le Tour de Santé* – the Tour of Health – and the start was held, symbollically, in Vittel, the town famous for its mineral water.

Doping didn't stop. Pills, potions and Pot Belge – a concoction containing a number of stimulants and pain suppressants – were used. But the consequences of being caught were not particularly serious.

In 1977, Bernard Thévenet won his second Tour a few months after testing positive at Paris-Nice. The following year, Michel Pollentier was kicked out of the Tour after taking the yellow jersey at Alpe d'Huez. I'd tried to picture how he cheated the dope test by concealing a bulb of fresh urine in his shorts and using a length of rubber tube to squirt it into the receptacle. Although he was removed from the Tour, Pollentier was racing again by the end of the season.

In 1988, Gert-Jan Theunisse tested positive for testosterone and was penalised ten minutes, dropping him from fourth place to 11th overall. Pedro Delgado, the winner, also tested positive, for a drug called probenicid, which was banned by the International Olympic Committee but not by the UCI.

Delgado was not penalized, keeping his yellow jersey. The message that gave out was very confusing.

Reading *Rough Ride*, by Paul Kimmage, in 1990 made everything clearer and by 1991, when the PDM team pulled out of the Tour, citing food poisoning, I was sceptical. Later we discovered PDM's riders had been given a dodgy batch of Intralipid, a nutritional substance given to patients unable to eat solids.

The early 1990s were a time of puzzling developments. There was the rebirth of Italian cycling, which had been in the doldrums, the rise of the sports doctor, the ONCE team's revolutionary preparation technique known as an 'active rest period', and then, in 1994, the ridiculous domination of the spring Classics by the Gewiss-Ballan team. Until then, I'd wondered if I was missing something, but watching three Gewiss riders drop the entire field to take first, second and third place at Flèche Wallonne looked very unusual. The significance of the fact the Gewiss team doctor's name was Michele Ferrari was not clear until later, but after that the role of EPO in cycling was on the agenda.

So when the Festina Affair happened, although it was shocking, it wasn't really a shock.

A week into the 1998 Tour, the decision was taken, belatedly, to throw the Festina team out of the race. With so much attention on them, the race's credibility was compromised. There were tears. Virenque reacted like a child who'd been told playtime was over, which, in a way, is exactly what he was.

Their claims of innocence seemed hollow but it is possible to look back and understand the sense of injustice. It could have been any one of a number of team cars that had been stopped and searched. The Festina riders were not the only ones doping but the complex code of silence required them to keep their mouths shut and watch the circus roll on without them. The bad-apple defence suited the Tour.

I took a day off work to watch the 15th stage, from Grenoble to Les Deux Alpes, which was broadcast in its entirety on Eurosport. I ignored my colleague at the newspaper when I heard him say: 'He's off on Monday. He's watching junkies race their bikes over mountains.'

The Tour does symbolism so well. That day the weather was filthy. The foreboding clouds seemed to be trying to suffocate the mountains, suppress the Tour even. And then Marco Pantani propelled himself forwards on the Galibier. He climbed like a helium balloon that had been let go and the defending champion, Jan Ullrich, was unable to respond. No one was able to respond.

In stark contrast to Pantani, Ullrich's body seemed to absorb the rain until he resembled a bloated, soggy pudding. Twelve months earlier, the German had looked set for a crushing, monotone Indurain-style era of dominance; now we had Pantani, the Tour's saviour in more ways than one, we thought.

But the Tour wasn't saved. Two days later, on the road to Aix-les-Bains, the race came the closest it had ever come to grinding to a halt.

The previous evening, riders from the TVM team were taken in for questioning by police convinced that doping did not begin and end with Festina. Rodolfo Massi, who seemed set to win the polka-dot jersey, was also arrested.

Although the TVM riders were released in time to start stage 17 in Albertville, Massi was still in custody. Incredibly, the Tour set off without its 'king of the mountains'.

The riders were unhappy. They refused to race and it took them well over an hour to reach the first intermediate sprint, 32 kilometres away. Then they stopped and sat in the road, protesting the involvement of the police. Tour boss Jean-Marie Leblanc tried to cajole the riders into continuing. There was an angry confrontation between Bjarne Riis, Manolo Saiz and Leblanc. Laurent Jalabert, the French champion, pulled out, followed by the rest of his ONCE team. A couple of others followed suit and the rest of the Spanish squads went home the next day.

Eventually the peloton rolled on towards Aix-les-Bains, where they arrived, hours behind schedule, to a muted reception. TVM's riders, perceived to have been wronged, were allowed to go to the front of the bunch to cross the line first.

That night, Leblanc – his goal no more ambitious

than reaching Paris and concluding the Tour – managed to persuade the rest of the teams to persevere. At the US Postal Service hotel, Frankie Andreu and his team-mates decided to indulge in larger-than-usual after-dinner ice creams, thinking that the Tour might rest where it stood.

But despite it all, the Tour went on.

1999

Looking back, it is interesting to note how the obstacles were removed from Lance Armstrong's path. In June, just as Pantani was about to clinch his second consecutive Giro d'Italia title, it was announced that he had failed a haematocrit test. There still wasn't an effective test to detect the use of exogenous EPO and the haematocrit ceiling remained the only tool the authorities had to curb its usage. Pantani's level was 52 per cent, two points above the limit. Because there was not a ratified test, being over the limit was not classed as a doping offence. Riders were rested, for the good of their health, for a fortnight before being allowed to race.

Having crushed his rivals at Madonna di Campiglio, extending his lead over Paolo Savoldelli to almost six minutes, Pantani was informed that his haematocrit was too high. Although a strong indication he had been using EPO, it could not be recorded as a water-tight doping case and to those who adored his style, it felt like he was being betrayed.

Then Ullrich pulled out of the Tour of Switzerland with an injured knee and announced he would not be fit for the Tour de France. Bearing in mind no one considered Armstrong a potential winner at that stage, the Tour had its weakest-looking field in years. The leading contender was Alex Zülle, who had just spent six months serving a suspension after admitting using EPO.

A couple of weeks before the Tour, I travelled to Paris for a press conference called by the Tour's organisers. They were dubbing it *le Tour de Renouveau* – the Tour of Renewal – and Leblanc was adopting a hard line. He announced his intention to bar Virenque, Teflon-coated Virenque, among others, from the race.

Cycling's peculiar form of justice meant the biggest losers in the fall-out from the Festina Affair was the Festina team itself because, although Brochard stayed put, the team lost its best two riders. Zülle accepted his six-month ban and resurfaced at Banesto, while Virenque kept squirming and joined the Italian Polti squad. It would take Virenque another year and a court appearance before he confessed.

Arriving at the Gare du Nord, I picked up a copy of his non-confessional *Ma Verité* (My Truth) – a sort of French art-house version of events that would later be renamed *Positively False* and made into a Hollywood blockbuster by Floyd Landis.

Leblanc's idea was a good one, but its application

was impractical, not least when the UCI announced
that it contravened the regulations. A race organiser
was not permitted to bar individual riders or teams
arbitrarily so close to the event. Virenque was back
in and, inevitably, he won his fifth king of the mountains title.

Having worked for *Cycling Weekly* for a year,
I'd heard enough stories of dopers, both proven
and unproven, and unprinted allegations of riders
buying and selling races, but nothing surprised or
disappointed me more than finding out that Tom
Simpson's legendary final utterance – 'Put me back
on my bike' – was invented by a journalist, Sid
Saltmarsh, who was miles away from Mont Ventoux
when the rider collapsed. There was something about
that which sat very uneasily.

Although I had ceased looking at the sport
through a fan's rose-tinted lenses, I arrived at the
Tour for the first time in 1999 and found the scale of
the event impressively bewildering. Everyone seemed
to know what they were doing and where they were
going. Except me.

I arrived after Sestrières, after *L'Equipe*'s oblique
yet damning headline, *Sur Une Autre Planète*, after
the news broke that Armstrong had tested positive
for corticosteroids following the prologue but had
produced a back-dated doctor's note to legitimise the
use, he said, of a saddle sore cream. The pace at which
the Tour moves, packing up overnight and moving

on, leaving barely a trace to suggest it had even been there, can happen to stories too. Events that seemed significant one day are squashed by the Tour's relentless, rolling narrative. Armstrong recognised that early on and he liked it that way. Before the Tour was even over, he had his line about 'never testing positive' so well rehearsed it was second nature. And while it's easy to accuse journalists of letting the positive-not positive story drop, it's also important to recognise that there was nothing further to go on at the time. No one realised the doctor's note had been falsified, or that Armstrong had been using the drug repeatedly and not to treat saddle sores. There were few dissenting voices. Both sides of the story were reported and the Tour moved on.

I met David Walsh on my second day at the Tour. Having admired his work, I embarrassed myself by saying so a little too quickly and enthusiastically. The studied indifference of the press corps didn't come easily to me. I then blurted out a question: 'Who do you think will win?'

'I'm not all that interested in who wins but how he does it,' came Walsh's reply.

I hadn't warmed to Armstrong, finding his brash manner unappealing, but I wasn't yet convinced of the need to be so sceptical. If he was doping, a year after the Festina Affair had almost brought the Tour to its knees, it would make him one of the most audacious and cynical cheats sport had ever known.

Covering the Tour as a first-timer, my goal was to ferret out a decent story. The day I arrived, a Belgian called Ludo Dierckxsens won the stage to Saint-Étienne. With his bald head and earring, he looked like Pantani. I discovered he had turned professional late, at the age of 30. Before that, he had worked at the DAF Trucks factory, spray-painting lorries. Now Belgian champion, and riding his first Tour, he'd won a stage. What a story.

I spoke to the Lampre team's press relations man and fixed up an interview with Dierckxsens. 'Come to the hotel tomorrow evening,' he said.

So I went and waited. The PR guy said he'd go and find Dierckxsens. Half an hour went by. 'He must be having a massage. He'll be down shortly,' said the PR guy, as he headed off for an evening bike ride.

There had still been no sign of Dierckxsens by the time the PR guy got back from his ride, so I went for a wander around the hotel. I asked anyone I saw in Lampre team issue clothing. I watched as the riders – minus Ludo – filed in for dinner. I watched as they came out again with satisfied stomachs while mine grumbled. I watched as the PR guy ignored my calls and disappeared down a corridor.

I'd been stood up, so, finally, I slipped away, tired and embarrassed to realise what a tiny, insignificant part of the Tour I was.

The next morning, the French papers had a story of a different kind. After his stage win, Dierckxsens was asked by the race doctor if he had taken any prescribed medication. He replied that he had used Synacthen, a corticoid, to treat a knee injury a few weeks earlier. Although he said he had a prescription, he had not told his team doctor, so the management sent him home.

When I saw the PR guy the following day, he was apologetic. I asked why he didn't just tell me that Dierckxsens was on his way home while I'd been waiting, pointlessly, in the hotel. He shrugged and said the management had been working on the wording of an official statement.

A few days later, Dierckxsens' test results came back negative. Had he said nothing to the race doctor, he would still have been in the Tour. After all, Armstrong had been able to excuse a positive result with a doctor's note. Dierckxsens' test had been negative, yet he had been sent home.

It was an early revelation that covering the Tour can be crazy and confusing. Black and white often blur until you see only grey. A story can be right under your nose, but if the wind is blowing the other way, there's no guarantee you'll get a whiff of it.

2000

It's Not About the Bike, Armstrong's inspirational tale of recovering from cancer to win the Tour, sold millions of copies. In America and Britain, in particular, Armstrong attracted people to cycling who had not previously been interested. In the book, he – or rather his ghostwriter Sally Jenkins – wrote: 'Drug testing was the most demeaning aspect of the Tour. Right after I finished a stage I was whisked away to an open tent where I sat in a chair while a doctor wrapped a piece of rubber tubing around my arm, jabbed me with a needle and drew blood. As I lay there, a battery of photographers flashed their cameras at me.'

He went on to explain that the drug tests proved he was clean. But there was something troubling about the detail. Blood tests were not conducted after stages and dope tests didn't take place in an open tent with photographers watching. I wrote about this at the time and still have the letter from a reader accusing me of looking for muck where there was none. In truth, this was tame scrutiny, no more than a simple attempt to hold a statement giving an inaccurate version of events up to the light.

With Pantani and Ullrich back, Armstrong was more bullish than ever. In 1999, he had held a press conference to try to convince the media he was clean. This time, when Daniel Baal, president of the French Cycling Federation, wondered out loud how Armstrong could be so much stronger than everyone else at Hautacam in the Pyrenees, the insinuation was clear, as was Armstrong's rebuttal: 'Prove it.'

That was the problem. Proving it. Even when French television filmed US Postal Service team staff disposing of packaging that was later discovered to contain Actovegin, a derivative of calves' blood that improves oxygen absorption, nothing stuck.

By now, the race for the yellow jersey interested me much less than the stories of suffering further back. Over the course of three weeks, I saw David Millar gradually disintegrate. The day he lost the yellow jersey following a chaotic team time trial by his Cofidis squad, he looked weary but his eyes were still bright. Ten days later, as I stood next to Tom Simpson's memorial on Mont Ventoux, I watched as Millar took off his cap and bowed his head. The next morning, in the start village in Avignon, his face looked drawn, as if he was being slowly drained of fight. I witnessed the brief, slightly awkward exchange he had with Simpson's daughter, who introduced herself and thanked him for his gesture. She placed into his hand a small fragment of the rock from the roadside, a memento. Millar put it in his pocket and, when she was out of earshot, said to me: 'What am I supposed to do with that? Carry it around with me for 200 kilometres?'

The next day I saw him again and he said: 'Part of me wanted to cry when she gave me that. If you see her, can you thank her for me?'

The Tour was exploiting the cracks in Millar. The next stage, to Briançon, was 249 kilometres, crossing the Col d'Allos, Col de Vars and Col d'Izoard. Millar was on the road for eight-and-a-half hours, and a traffic jam meant his team spent another five hours in the bus trying to get to their hotel. Angry at the demands being placed on him, Millar sought out Jean-Marie Leblanc to tell him.

On the final day, Millar honoured a promise he had made to himself by attacking on the Champs-Élysées. He was determined to show the Tour could not break him. That would come later.

2001

Armstrong's relationship with the French was never warm. And he had a knack of rubbing them up the wrong way.

At the time, it was explained as a mere coincidence, but after the French passed a series of anti-doping laws, Armstrong moved from Nice to Girona in Spain. And, early in the year, he did something that seemed deliberately provocative. He released his racing programme and there was not a single French race on it bar the Tour. I wrote an opinion piece suggesting that the French might see it as a snub, and that he might even be booed at the *Grand Départ* in Dunkirk.

For all his skill at manipulating people, Armstrong never really understood the French public. He believed that victory silenced doubters and won friends. He didn't appreciate that the French have a complex relationship with sporting figures. For example, they were cool towards Jacques

Anquetil, who won five Tours, but adored Raymond Poulidor, who won none.

When the US Postal team was presented in Dunkirk, there were a few boos. It was only a minority, but for the reigning Tour champion to be greeted by even isolated jeers seemed unthinkable then.

2003

I stopped writing about cycling in late 2001 and went and worked for newspapers for a couple of years. It would be disingenuous to say that I left *Cycling Weekly* because I couldn't stomach Armstrong's dominance. I did not believe the fairytale, but there was more to it than that.

The Tour was in danger of losing its storytelling charm. It had become a blockbuster in which only the star mattered. Everyone else was reduced to the role of supporting actor. Stage winners were a sideshow, the yellow jersey was sent out on loan, then reeled in when it suited him. Being a contrarian, I wanted to see him beaten, or at least challenged.

The centenary Tour offered a glimmer of hope. Armstrong was below his best and vulnerable, Ullrich was rejuvenated and handed out perhaps the only significant beating in a seven-year stretch by winning the time trial at Cap' Découverte on a baking-hot afternoon. There was drama, too, when Armstrong was forced to go cross-country to avoid falling on the descent into Gap when Joseba Beloki swerved, wobbled and fell sickeningly hard. And again at Luz Ardiden when his handlebars caught a spectator's bag and he went down. But each time he got up.

2005

Flanked by Ivan Basso and Jan Ullrich, after his record seventh Tour victory, Lance Armstrong provided the last word. Lance always liked to have the last word. 'To the people who don't believe in cycling, the cynics and sceptics, I'm sorry you don't believe in miracles. You should believe in these athletes and you should believe in these people. There are no secrets – this is a hard sporting event and hard work wins it.'

2006

It's funny how the weather seems to amplify the drama of the Tour at key times. In Strasbourg, on the evening of the team presentation, the skies darkened and thunder rumbled in the distance. That was the sound of Operación Puerto moving ever closer.

For a month, the rumours had been solidifying. A blood-doping ring, run by Madrid-based gynaecologist Dr Eufemiano Fuentes, had been discovered by Spanish police. They had apprehended Manolo Saiz, he of the 'active rest periods', now the boss of the Liberty Seguros team, with a suitcase full of cash. A search of Dr Fuentes's lab uncovered blood bags said to contain the blood of half the peloton.

In this, the first Tour *sans* Lance, the battle for the yellow jersey appeared to be a straight fight between the two men who had battled, in vain, to topple him: Ullrich and Basso. We were about to discover that both men were clients of the same blood-doping doctor. The absurdity of it was striking. How do you seek a competitive advantage by both paying the same doctor?

Before the presentation in Strasbourg, the teams sailed down the river to meet a crowd unaware of just how alarmingly things had escalated. Names were being named. T-Mobile were so concerned about the risk to its reputation that the team management had asked their riders to sign a document guaranteeing they were not involved.

One by one the teams were introduced. As they filtered off the stage into the area where the TV crews and journalists were waiting, Basso and Ullrich both quickened their stride, side-stepped the interviews and were spirited away. That night, it rained heavily, and next morning both Ullrich and Basso went home. Unfortunately, it took a lot more than a heavy shower to cleanse that Tour.

Basso's team boss, Bjarne Riis, resorts to arrogance under fire. He puffs out his chest and keeps his responses short. It was unfortunate for Riis that his CSC team was staying in a hotel just a short walk from the huge conference centre that housed the Tour's press room for the opening weekend.

Surrounded by journalists and cameramen, it took Riis a good 20 minutes to make the walk from his hotel to the conference centre. When he got there, he had no answers. He explained that sending Basso home was not an admission of guilt. Instead, he'd been sent home so he could concentrate on clearing his name. The logic was typically twisted.

A few days into the race, with rumours that a 'second' list was about to be circulated, the fear was palpable around the start village. One morning, a rider said: 'Rider X is terrified. He's spending half his time back at the team car and thinks the police are going to be waiting at the finish line.' I have chosen not to name either rider because I do not have a shorthand note or recording of the conversation, but it happened.

A few weeks before the Tour, just as Operación Puerto was breaking, I interviewed Floyd Landis and his coach, Allen Lim, about the technicalities of mountain climbing in the Tour. Lim spoke with zeal and a scientist's clarity. He went into detail about the watts Landis was able to produce and how he tackled the climbs. I asked about the doping in cycling and he said: 'That just is not an issue with us.'

Landis was amiable but wanted to get something off his chest. 'Those guys at *VeloNews* did a whole issue on drugs… Do they think everyone is doing it? I would hate for anyone to think I'm doing it.'

Noting Landis's good form – he'd won Paris-

Nice and the Tour of California – I'd stuck a speculative £40 on him to win the Tour. His odds with the online bookmaker were generous: 50/1.

With Basso and Ullrich out of the race, that began to look like a pretty decent bet.

We all know the story of the fall of Floyd Landis. We now know that he doped at US Postal and had continued at Phonak. We can speculate that had Armstrong offered him a place on his team in 2009 instead of freezing him out, the Texan might not have fallen at all. It was Landis's sense of injustice at seeing Armstrong come back while he was in the margins that set the dominoes toppling.

Having suffered a terrible half-hour at La Toussuire, Landis lost the yellow jersey and, seemingly, any chance of winning the 2006 Tour.

The 17th stage from St-Jean-de-Maurienne to Morzine, the final Alpine stage, was his last opportunity to get back into contention before the time trial. By any objective measure, he had no chance.

It was one of those days where everything went wrong for us. We got stuck on the *autoroute* and were in danger of missing everything, so we decided there was nothing for it but to find a bar with a television.

By now, Landis was powering on alone. The first thing that struck me was how many bottles of water he was taking from the team car. I wondered if there was an old-fashioned form of cheating going on, with Landis benefitting from the old 'sticky bottle'.

A friend, watching at his home in the south of France, sent a text.

'What do you make of this?'

Reluctant to cast aspersions without proof, and perhaps remembering Landis's words to me a few weeks earlier, I was diplomatic.

'It's either the greatest comeback in Tour history, or it's not.'

Landis closed to within 30 seconds of Oscar Pereiro, who had inherited the yellow jersey at La Toussuire. In the final time trial, he completed the miraculous comeback. It should have been one of the great sport stories but something didn't ring true.

Almost as soon as the Tour was over, the rumours started. When Landis cancelled a lucrative post-Tour criterium appearance in the Netherlands, the story slotted into place. The Tour winner had failed a dope test and I kept pressing refresh on my online banking account to see if my 'winnings' had been paid.

2007

Towards the end of stage five to Autun, Alexandre Vinokourov crashed on a bend and injured both knees badly. For one of the favourites, it was the worst possible time to fall, just as things were hotting up at the front. Half a dozen of his Astana team-mates waited for him and the train of riders in baby blue tried to drag him back to the peloton. It was a painful and, ultimately, unsuccessful chase.

Vinokourov crossed the line over a minute after the bunch, grimacing, with blood weeping from both knees and running down his shins. He went straight to hospital and had both wounds stitched. The stitches had been left a little looser than would usually be the case so they wouldn't burst as he pedalled. Vinokourov was not conceding defeat.

This was the Tour – an event that pushes people beyond their limits. Riders have soldiered on with broken bones and diarrhoea, refusing to quit until they have reached the point of no return.

Next morning, in Semur-en-Auxois, I watched Vinokourov hobble up the steps to sign on. Both knees were bandaged, as was one elbow. Fine gauze netting held the bandages in place. He looked like he was in the process of being mummified. He could barely walk. Each step forced him to scrunch his face up in pain. The idea of him completing the 200 kilometres to Bourg-en-Bresse seemed inconceivable.

But he survived that day. And the next. He finished in the same group as the overall contenders at Le Grand Bornand the day after that but the suffering became too much on the second mountain stage, to Tignes, and he slipped back. After the first rest day, any hope of winning the Tour was gone but his tears at the finish only endeared him further to the public. The Tour had its side story of heroism, stoicism and masochism.

Michael Rasmussen took the yellow jersey in

Tignes but by the time the race reached the south of France, his hold on it was beginning to look tenuous. There had been reports that he had missed out-of-competition dope tests and that he – like Vinokourov – had been training in plain kit to avoid being spotted when the testers came calling. The UCI's head of anti-doping, Anne Gripper, had dubbed them 'The Men in Black'. Things were unravelling fast.

The media scrum was particularly tight outside the Rabobank team bus in Montpellier. The usual routine of denying everything until the facts are utterly irrefutable was in full swing.

At Albi, Astana and Rabobank were staying in the same Campanile hotel, an unremarkable place on the outskirts of town that was made notable by the fact that one of the buildings just across the road from the car park was a blood transfusion centre. We laughed at that. It was only a coincidence but we liked to imagine the Tour's organisers were having a little joke to themselves too.

The time trial around Albi was crucial to Rasmussen's chances of winning the Tour. The Dane had been in the yellow jersey since Tignes and, with the Pyrenees to come, was beginning to look like a potential champion, although racing solo against the clock had always been his *bête noire*.

Rasmussen cut a strange figure that morning. Thin to the point of being skeletal, oddly pale considering he'd been riding his bike in the sunshine for weeks, he bore more than a passing resemblance to the figure in Edvard Munch's The Scream. On time-trial days, the riders often take the opportunity to sleep in and breakfast late. Rasmussen, as the last man to set off that afternoon, had most of the day to kill, so it had just gone noon by the time he came down to eat his porridge and omelette. As he entered the dining room, the last three of his team-mates got up and left together, with barely a nod of acknowledge-ment between them. It added to the impression that Rasmussen was a loner – an isolated figure even in his own team.

Time trials in the Tour can be funny days. They are tense, rather than exciting, but the stages them-selves often reveal more about the key protagonists in just 40 or 50 kilometres than the days in the high mountains that capture the imagination.

They call it 'the race of truth' but that day the time trial seemed to fib to us repeatedly. Vinokourov won and Rasmussen did the ride of his life to keep the yellow jersey.

Later, we sat in the sunshine in the car park and waited for the men of the day to return. A Rabobank car arrived and pulled up as close to the hotel's back door as possible so Rasmussen could avoid the crowds and slip inside. A little later, the Astana car arrived. What followed was pure pantomime.

The car parked on the far side, leaving Vinok-ourov with a longer walk. He swung his legs out of the passenger seat footwell like a patient returning home after an operation and then walked slowly, agonisingly across the car park. This was a man who had just beaten the Tour de France in a 54-kilometre time trial?

That evening at dinner, my colleague sent a text message to Pat McQuaid, the president of the UCI: 'This sport is a joke.'

'We're working on it,' he replied.

Two days later, Vinokourov won a gruelling mountain stage over the Port de Larrau, Col de Marie-Blanque and Col d'Aubisque. We were being asked to believe in miracles.

The rest day in Pau turned out to be crazier and more exhilarating than any other during that race. It started in the cool, grand surroundings of the Palais de Beaumont, where Rasmussen, the *maillot jaune*, held a press conference.

The fragile-looking figure shuffled in and took his place at the top table. He sat down next to his team manager, Theo De Rooy. On the other side of De Rooy was Harro Knijff, the Rabobank team's lawyer. How many riders bring their lawyer to a press conference?

Rasmussen started with a statement. He had made a mistake about declaring his whereabouts for being available for out-of-competition dope testing, he had received a written warning from the UCI and had apologised.

It was, he explained, an administrative error. 'I am sorry this situation is coming up now, while I am wearing the yellow jersey, because it's harming the sport I love,' he said. They never forget to mention how much they love the sport.

The story became more convoluted as Rasmussen lost track of the details under questioning. An allegation that he'd asked for a shoebox full of drugs to be sent from the United States to Italy five years earlier resurfaced. He denied it, urging everyone to focus on the race.

Then came a question that seemed to stop him in his tracks.

'Do you understand why no one believes you?'

Later it emerged that while he was supposed to have been in Mexico – Rasmussen's wife was Mexican – he had actually been in Italy. Not only that, but Davide Cassani, an Italian professional turned television commentator, had seen him. The game was up.

Astonishingly, Rasmussen had a reprieve for a day or so because while the tangled knot of lies and half-truths was still being unpicked, news came through that Vinokourov had tested positive. Rarely has the press room emptied so fast – not even when word gets round that the buffet is running out.

By the time we reached La Palmeraie, a smart hotel a little way out of Pau, Vinokourov had left and the place was swarming with gendarmes, their guns rocking threateningly on their hips as they marched about the place collecting bags and cases.

There was plenty of opportunity for comic relief. At one point, the team's press officer made an announcement that Marc Biver, the Astana team boss, would speak to the media if we would all gather in the garden at the rear of the hotel. All but a handful of the reporters and cameramen present jostled and barged their way through a small gate and into the garden, leaving me and a few other sceptical souls to witness the remainder of the Astana riders leaving by the hotel's main entrance before getting wordlessly into the cars and driving away.

By then it was obvious nothing much was going to happen, but we hung around for another hour or so just in case. I scrawled a note – a pretty weak joke at the Kazakh team's expense – on a page of my pad and stuck it under the windscreen-wiper of the last remaining Astana car: 'Borat hates dopers.' A photographer took a shot of it and the following day I saw the image in one of the French papers.

The next day, Rasmussen won the summit finish at the Col d'Aubisque to seemingly seal the Tour.

Having decided to stay in Pau rather than get caught in the inevitable traffic jam on the mountain, I heard the TV commentator say that the Cofidis rider Cristian Moreni had tested positive for testosterone and would be met by police at the finish line.

I drove to the Novotel where Cofidis were staying and waited. News filtered through that the other

Cofidis riders were being escorted down the mountain by police and would have their rooms searched. The hotel was closed to the public and was roped off with plastic tape as if it were a crime scene.

When Bradley Wiggins arrived, he had the look on his face of a small boy who had no idea what he might be caught up in. His room was searched, the contents of his washbag were rifled through, and when we spoke later he sounded shaken.

But we were not done yet. It was gone 11pm when the call came to drive to the Rabobank hotel. With just four days to go to Paris the team pulled Rasmussen out of the race, handing victory to Alberto Contador. Johan Bruyneel, Contador's boss, happily, absurdly, claimed an eighth Tour victory.

* * *

The years since have not been without controversy. The 2008 race was blighted by positive tests for Riccardo Riccò, Leonardo Piepoli, Stefan Schumacher and Bernhard Kohl, who won five stages and the king of the mountains title between them.

Riccò's performances were preposterous. He was like a moustache-twiddling baddie who thought he was above comeuppance, but watching Kohl made us wonder whether the clean-up was having the desired effect. Were new riders, previously unable to compete, being allowed to come through?

Kohl's positive test for CERA, a new-generation EPO, undermined any temptation to believe that doper-detection was a matter of gut instinct. It was impossible not to feel sadness on learning that he had been doping since the age of 19.

Alberto Contador tested positive for clenbuterol during the 2010 Tour. Although detected only in tiny quantities, clenbuterol is not a substance that occurs naturally in the body so it had to get there by artificial means. Contador argued it was in some beef he ate but the rules of strict liability meant that how it got there was of no consequence.

The legal and scientific argument went on for months and so Contador was free to line up for the 2011 Tour knowing that he could win it and be stripped of that title as well as the 2010 one.

Riis was at his most arrogant, claiming that as Contador was free to race, he was only respecting the rules. After a tense pre-race press conference, I stepped forward to ask Riis: 'You talk about following the rules but you didn't follow the rules in 1996. What's changed?' Riis did not reply. Instead he glared his icy-blue glare and kept walking.

You could argue that the era since 1998 has been the dirtiest in the sport's history, but it might be more accurate to say it's been the most transparent. The evolution of doping in cycling is not an unbroken line, it is a continuous progression. The substances changed and became more effective, the methods more sophisticated, but if EPO had been available in any previous era, there would have been riders prepared to take it in order to gain an edge.

Paradoxically, the grubbiest-looking era is perhaps responsible for the most significant cultural shift.

After the fall of Armstrong, the roll of honour has been left blank from 1999 to 2005 – and rightly so – but if the same questions were asked of the race's entire history, how many names would be left?

What is apparent is that the Tour de France is not only one of the toughest sporting events in the world, it is also the most resilient. The scandals and the disappointments are, like the riders themselves, transient. They come and go. And, if a seven-time winner can be stripped of his titles, who's to say how indelible the roll of honour is?

I used to think that the riders owed it to the Tour, and to the fans, to be outspoken against doping and demonstrably clean. But that is not true. They owe it only to themselves. Because the Tour will endure no matter how many charlatans attempt to appropriate its yellow jersey. The Tour will outlive them all.

Lionel Birnie first covered the Tour for *Cycling Weekly* in 1999. In recent years he has written for *The Sunday Times*. He photographed every meal he ate on Tour in 2012 for a blog called Le Gourmet de France. He wasn't sure what to make of the fact more people read that than his analysis of the race. He collaborated with Sean Kelly on his autobiography, *Hunger,* and with Rob Hayles on *My Life on a Bike.*

13

Beyond the polished exterior of the Tour de France, there is a man – hard, but fair; fearsome, yet amiable – who keeps the wheels of the race rolling.

James Startt meets Jean-François Pescheux, the race director, who plays a major role in designing the route and, during the race itself, rules with an iron fist.

Pescheux ended his pro career aged 29 to join the organisation. The 100th Tour will be his final one before retirement.

THE DIRECTOR

BY JAMES STARTT

'The kid just didn't get it!' Jean-François Pescheux laughs after getting out of his red Tour de France car.

On hand at a junior team time trial race held in conjunction with the Tour de l'Avenir in August, Pescheux spent the morning observing the different squads. And when he saw the strongest rider on one outfit dropping all of his team-mates, he attempted to give the adolescent a little on-the-road advice.

'I drove up and said, "You may be the strongest, but in this event you're no stronger than your team-mates. You need to slow down a little and your team could have a faster overall time." But the kid just looked at me, put his head down and kept going!' Pescheux grins.

One can only wonder what the teenage champion-to-be thought when the Tour de France race director was suddenly at his side. Quite likely he did not even understand who Pescheux was.

Most people, of course, associate the Tour de France with Christian Prudhomme, the general director and major spokesman in car number one. But, as race director, Pescheux is the man who runs the race from the inside out, the voice from the back of the peloton in car number two.

And what a voice it is! Sometimes Pescheux is simply low-key and informative as he watches over the riders, the photographers' motorcycles and the cars full of team officials, race guests and journalists. Almost nonchalantly, he will alert a team car when a rider raises a hand to ask for water bottles, a bicycle change or some tactical advice.

But let Pescheux spot an infraction – a car driving dangerously, a motorcycle offering a draft or a rider stopped on the wrong (left) side of the road – and his voice takes on a growl, followed quickly by an exclamation. The mildest one, translated from French, is 'It's not possible.' Next in severity is 'Stop! You have no business there.' Finally he barks at an offender, 'Come see me after the stage.' His tone is: 'Vengeance will be mine.' He has the power to expel cars and motorcycles from the race, and occasionally exercises it for a stage or two.

'It can get crazy sometimes,' he says. 'There are moments in each race where everybody wants to be in the same place at the same time.' His job is to make sure that doesn't happen. He does that so well that, while he can sound surly, he is highly respected.

'Jean-François follows everything in cycling. He knows everyone from the cadets to the top pros, and he knows everything there is to know when it comes to the race rules,' says Marc Madiot, the manager of the Française des Jeux team. 'He is one of the great minds of the sport.'

Pescheux learned his trade from his predecessor as race director, the equally volatile Albert Bouvet. A common joke is that Pescheux's main qualification for the job was his ability to match Bouvet in magnitude of screaming.

'Albert was my mentor,' Pescheux explains. 'He was a hard man. He was a rock cutter before in Brittany, a real hard worker that knew how to be respected. He was really tough, but always human.'

In many ways, including their deep love of the sport, Pescheux is cut from the same cloth.

'Jean-François is the good cop and the bad cop all wrapped into one,' says Jean-Marie Leblanc, who worked with Pescheux as Tour de France director from 1988 until 2005.

'On race radio he is very rigorous. In the middle of a race, he doesn't joke around. The job requires such strictness. But afterwards, yes he does. He looks at life positively, and in a team you need people like that. That was a huge advantage in the years we worked together. He could always put things in perspective and keep morale high.'

Both Leblanc and Pescheux look back on their years working together with fondness. In that time, the Tour de France was only just beginning to transform itself into the big business it is today. Together, the two would often outline the following year's race route on a napkin over lunch.

'Back then we organised the race from A to Z,' Pescheux remembers. 'We even took care of booking the team hotels. Now it is much more specialised, and I just focus on the race itself. But in the beginning, I would be at the printer on the Friday before each race, printing out the road book.'

Like Bouvet and Leblanc, Pescheux is a former professional rider who rode for the Jobo and La Redoute teams in the 1970s and early 1980s.

'When I was a professional, I was general secretary of the riders' union – the Union Nationale des Cyclistes Professionnels. After a meeting in 1981, Albert Bouvet and Félix Lévitan [the Tour director at the time] came to see me and asked if I would be interested in joining the Tour. "When?" I asked, since I had just re-signed a three-year contract with La Redoute. "As soon as possible!" they said.

'I told them I'd think about it – and decided to join them. I was 29 years old. If I rode out my contract, I would be 32, and then what? I was not interested in becoming a team director. "The Tour de France is the summit," I thought, and began work on January 1, 1982.'

For the first decade, he worked as a race regulator from a motorcycle.

'You know, when I was on a motorbike, Jean-

Marie once said to me, "Jean-François, take off your race number. You're not a racer any more!" We laughed but that was the way I was, always close to the race. And then in 1994, when Jean-Marie asked me to direct the race from the car after Albert retired I said, "Okay, but in race car number two, behind the race." That's the place I always wanted, behind the peloton. That's where everything happens. That's the heart of the race.'

French cycling hero Bernard Hinault raced with Pescheux as a professional, and now works with him on the Tour as a member of the public relations department.

'Jean-François was never a great champion,' says Hinault, squarely, but without insult. And compared to the five-time Tour de France winner, Pescheux could barely be defined as a champion. After all, his collection of professional victories starts with a stage win in the Circuit de la Sarthe and ends with the now defunct Nice-Alassio. But Pescheux's limits as a rider proved to be qualities as a race director.

'To get the most out of his talent, he had to see all aspects of a race,' Hinault says. 'And that is a huge quality to have in a race director. He is passionate about bike racing. He's also trained as a race official, so he knows all of the rules inside and out. When it comes down to it, I don't think there is anyone out there who can teach Jean-François anything about a bike race.'

More than the Tour de France, more than great races like Paris-Roubaix, Pescheux insists he simply loves bicycle racing. And throughout the year he can be seen at a host of smaller races, be it the Tour de l'Avenir – symbolically the amateur Tour de France – or the local race put on by his old amateur club US Nemours St Pierre, held each year on the Monday after Easter.

When he's not watching races, he's designing them, with visits to the roads set to be used by the Tour stages, checking out turns and climbs. Sometimes he needs days to inspect a single stage.

Pescheux insists that the job of race director in itself is not hard. But the tension and constant pressure build up. And he admits that on more than one occasion he has taken a race to bed with him afterwards.

'I remember when everybody crashed on the stage into Spa, in Belgium, during the 2010 Tour,' Pescheux says. 'That night, I didn't sleep. I was asking myself questions: "Should I have neutralised the race?" After the crash, it took me ten minutes to drive back up to the front of the race. People were just everywhere! At one point we passed Robbie McEwen and blood was just spurting out! Afterwards I thought, "What if that was more serious? What if he had collapsed and died?" That would have been on my shoulders! Such situations do not happen often, but it is my responsibility.'

Undoubtedly the worst moment as race director came in the 1995 Tour when a young Olympic champion, Fabio Casartelli, was killed in the Pyrenees after crashing on the descent of the Portet d'Aspet, just 34 kilometres into stage 15.

'Casartelli's death was my worst day as race director,' Pescheux recalls. 'We were one of the first cars to pass him, and we understood right away that it was serious. Normally when we pass after a crash guys are picking themselves up. But Fabio was just lying there, immobile in a foetal position. Then we learned from the radio that he was being evacuated by helicopter. Then we learned that he had died. First the doctors told us that he was clinically dead, but they were still trying to animate him. Finally they said there was nothing they could do.

'But we didn't want to announce it right away. We couldn't! We were trying to call the family first and let them know, but riders were coming up and asking what was going on. There were still more than 100 kilometres of racing to go. The problem was that we were still in the race but we weren't in the race. It was terrible.'

Pescheux also says he is nervous any day a public protest is announced along the race route. France is known for its countless *manifestations* – demonstrations – every year. Some can be almost light-hearted as a union or workers let off steam against an employer or their working conditions. There have been some to protest against the killing of wild wolves, while others lament the killing of livestock by the same wolves. Either way, slowing the Tour down always provides added visibility to the cause. But on occasion the *manifs* threaten to sabotage the Tour.

'The problem with the protests is you never know which way they are going to turn,' he says. 'It's always stressful.'

Although he feels that good moments are to be had on a daily basis on the Tour, he insists that the best day is always the last, when the pack rolls into Paris safe and sound and makes its way up and down the Champs-Élysées.

'There is nothing better than when the riders come up to me after the race on the Champs-Élysées and thank me for a good race. That's real happiness for me.'

This year, Pescheux sets off on his 19th Tour de France as race director. It will also be his last, as he's retiring, at the age of 61. Replacing him will be another former professional, Thierry Gouvenou. Like Pescheux, Gouvenou had a modest racing career, and, like Pescheux, he is passionate about all aspects of bike racing, and understands the challenge that awaits him.

'Jean-François is a real character, not only in France but around the world,' Gouvenou says. 'He just knows everything there is to know about the sport. And he knows the rules inside and out. That is so important because, when you make a call, you can't get it wrong.'

Gouvenou, however, is distinctly unlike Pescheux in one way: Gouvenou is reserved, discreet by nature. Pescheux's protégé insists that the positions he takes are more important than the way he voices them.

'The important thing is to be firm, but fair,' says Gouvenou.

After all, actions speak louder than words.

James Startt has covered the Tour de France and other international bicycle races for 23 years, and is the author of the first English history of the Tour de France entitled, *Tour de France/Tour de Force* (Chronicle Books), as well as numerous other cycling-related books. His photographs are distributed by Agence Zoom and are exhibited by the Agathe Gaillard Gallery, the oldest photography gallery in France. He has worked as the European Associate for *Bicycling* magazine since 1999. Living in Paris, he currently holds the title, Our Man In Europe, for *Bicycling*.

14

Daniel Lloyd was beginning
to think his dream of riding the
Tour was going to pass him by.

Then, with just over a week to go
before the start of the 2010 race,
he was called up to replace an
injured Cervélo team-mate.

Lloyd's job was to support both
Carlos Sastre and Thor Hushovd
as they competed for the yellow
and green jerseys.

What's it really like to ride the
Tour? This is his account of how
he became a giant of the road.

A DOMESTIQUE'S TALE

BY DANIEL LLOYD

Do·mes·tique
Servant. In professional cycling; a team helper.

When my phone rang, I glanced at the screen to see who was calling before answering.

Jean-Paul, it said.

I felt a lump in my throat, my stomach tightened and a few connected thoughts flashed through my mind. Jean-Paul Van Poppel was my sports director. There was just over a week to go before the Tour de France was due to start in Rotterdam. My Cervélo team-mate Heinrich Haussler had been struggling with injury after a crash at the Tour of Switzerland. And I was first reserve.

I knew that the next few moments would mean either the realisation of a childhood dream or crushing disappointment.

I answered the phone and braced myself.

* * *

This is not the story of a superstar. There's not much glamour in suffering but if you want to read the story of a fan who climbed far enough up the ladder to get the opportunity to ride the greatest race in the world, stick with me.

In 2010, I had the privilege of suffering through the Tour de France. I mean it when I describe it as a privilege, and here's why. Each July only a couple of hundred people get the chance to ride the Tour. To get to the Tour, a cyclist first has to be good enough to turn professional, then earn a contract with one of the top teams and finally make the cut when management pick their final nine for the race.

When I told people I was a professional cyclist, they always asked the same question. They still do.

Have you ridden the Tour de France?

I wasn't embarrassed to say, 'No, but I have ridden the Giro d'Italia,' but I wanted one day to be able to give a different answer.

By June 2010, I was beginning to think my career would take me tantalisingly close to the Tour without actually enabling me to achieve the dream. I knew I could never win a race like the Tour – I wasn't a fantasist – but to pin the number to my back and be part of it was within my reach. I also knew, given a fair chance, I could make it to Paris and become one of the giants of the road. I was like a kid with his nose pressed up against the window of a toyshop, wondering whether I'd get the invitation to go inside. I was six weeks shy of my 30th birthday. And I was absolutely knackered.

To put my story into context, I should explain

how I reached the professional ranks in the first place, how I had been plugging away for years, not without success exactly, but living in hope, rather than expectation, that my big break would come.

At the age of 13, I took part in my first race – a mountain bike race at Matchams Park near where I grew up in Dorset, southern England. My first road race was the 1998 Junior Tour of Wales and my first experience of international road racing came three years later in France. Rod Ellingworth, who now works as Team Sky's race coach, fixed me up with a place at a club called UVCA Troyes in eastern France. Rod had raced for them for a few seasons and he put in a good word, so from July to September I shared a flat with my team-mate Russell Downing and got stuck in. The following year, I moved south to Clermont-Ferrand to join a club called CO Chamalières.

In 2003, I joined Endurasport, a small British team based in Italy and run by the former professional rider Harry Lodge. Harry did a bloody good job running a team on half a shoestring and he cobbled together a decent racing programme that gave me my first experience of racing against the proper professionals. At my first top-level race, the Coppa Agostoni in northern Italy, I was in awe of the riders around me. There was Oscar Camenzind, a former world champion, Francesco Casagrande, Ivan Basso and Danilo Di Luca. As I climbed the stairs to the podium to sign on before the race, I followed

Casagrande, who was the eventual winner of the race. The rapturous applause from the crowd was one thing but the thing that struck me was the definition in Casagrande's calf muscles. His legs looked to be covered in skin no thicker than tissue paper. I'd never seen anything like it before.

I'd heard the stories of the pros riding at 55 or 60 kilometres an hour on the flat, but I thought it must be an exaggeration until that day. As we sped through the urban streets at the start of the race, I had to get out of the saddle and sprint to hold my place in the line. It was so fast that I was worried the rider in front – a skinny-looking climber – might not be able to hold the wheel. I had my fingers crossed because I knew if he allowed the gap to open, there was no way I'd be able to close it.

Just as I was thinking that, he took one hand off his bars, reached down to his bottle and took a long swig from it. He wasn't about to drop the wheel; he wasn't even suffering. I already knew I had a long way to go, but that moment drilled it home.

I climbed the ladder in small steps. My next step was upwards, but not by much. I spent two years with Flanders-Afin, a small Belgian-based squad in the UCI's division three, the equivalent of a 'Continental' pro team now. The highlight of both seasons was riding the Three Days of De Panne, which takes place the week before the Tour of Flanders, and so is a hubbub of excitement. Our team could not afford hotels, or, if they could, felt it was a waste of money. After the first stage, we went back home, more than 100 kilometres away, cooked for ourselves, washed our bikes and kit and woke early the next morning so we could be picked up to drive 100 kilometres back to De Panne for stage two. They don't do that at Quick Step.

In 2006, I rode in Asia for the Giant team and finished fourth in the Tour of Qinghai Lake, one of the biggest races in China. That got me a place with the DFL-Cyclingnews team back in Europe for 2007. We had Nico Mattan on the team, which earned us invitations to some of the big races in Belgium. Then I spent a year with the Irish An Post team, which has since developed a reputation for helping riders move on to World Tour-level squads, notably Matt Brammeier, Andy Fenn and Gediminas Bagdonas.

The reason for sharing my biography is to show how difficult it was to make progress. I knew I wasn't earmarked for greatness, but I was doing my best. I wasn't a prolific winner, but I worked hard and always gave what I had. I loved the sport and, when I wasn't racing, I watched everything I could on television. I dreamed of one day being able to rub shoulders with the riders I saw on television. I dreamed of being one of them.

At 28, married, with a child, and earning very little money, it was beginning to feel like it would remain a dream rather than my destiny.

In late 2008, I got a call from Brian Smith, the former British champion, who was helping to set up the new Cervélo team, sponsored by the Canadian bicycle manufacturer. It seemed they were interested in signing me. I was very excited but I couldn't allow myself to get my hopes up. My career – if I could loosely describe it as such – had been more downs than ups at that point. Plenty of promises had gone unfulfilled.

The contract came good and so I allowed myself to dream once more. During my debut season, I rode, and finished, the Giro d'Italia. I was a *domestique* – a worker bee – and my duties were to the team, and particularly our leaders Carlos Sastre and Thor Hushovd.

I fetched clothing and water bottles from the team car, I stopped when the leaders needed to pee and paced them back to the bunch, I gave them my wheels when they punctured. And I was happy doing it. A job well done gave me a tremendous amount of satisfaction. Sometimes I was able to play a tactical role, getting into a break to relieve the pressure on my team. One of the most memorable days was at the 2009 Tour of Flanders. To spend 40 kilometres off the front in one of my favourite races, with Sylvain Chavanel, was the stuff I'd been dreaming about.

By 2010 I felt I had found my feet at the top level. My team-mates and the management seemed to appreciate the work I'd done. Perhaps because I was easy-going, always willing to work hard and rarely complained, I got selected for more and more races.

The start of the 2010 season was like being on a conveyor belt. Starting at the Etoile de Bessèges in the south of France, I went to the Tour of Oman, then Het Volk, Paris-Nice and the full menu of Belgian Classics and semi-Classics – Dwars door Vlaanderen, the Grand Prix E3 Harelbeke, Ghent-Wevelgem, the Tour of Flanders and the Grand Prix Pino Cerami. After a short break, I finished the Giro again, then, with just six days' rest after the Giro, went to the Critérium du Dauphiné in the French Alps because the team needed me to fill their roster.

I didn't finish the Dauphiné – I packed it on the last day to Sallanches. I'd almost quit two days before that, but I wanted to do the stage to Alpe d'Huez, so I suffered on. I was totally drained, and felt like I needed a break to recharge my batteries and recover for the second half of the season.

So, when Jean-Paul rang about a week after the Dauphiné and suggested I do the Tour of Austria in July, I protested, and pleaded with him to let me take a break. He agreed, and took Austria off my programme. My last race before my break was the National Championships in Lancashire, and I was rooming with my Cervélo team-mate Jeremy Hunt.

Jez had spoken to Heinrich Haussler, who doubted he would be fit for the Tour following a crash with Mark Cavendish at the Tour of Switzerland. It was beginning to look like Cervélo would need to call up one of their reserves to take Heino's place, and I was starting to wish I hadn't told Jean-Paul I felt so tired. After all, if I said I was too drained to ride the Tour of Austria, they were hardly likely to put me in the hardest race in the world, were they?

That is why I answered the phone call from Jean-Paul with such trepidation. Was The Opportunity going to be offered? Or was this a courtesy call to let me down gently?

'Dan, I'm not sure how much you've heard, but Heino's having a lot of trouble with his knee. The doctors don't think he's up to racing the Tour. We've discussed things with Thor and Carlos, and we'd like you to replace him.'

Inside I was delighted, but tried not to show it to Jean-Paul. I put the phone down and turned to Jez.

'I'm in… Should I do it?'

I was exhausted, and I was worried about making a fool of myself on the biggest stage in the world. I didn't want to show up the team or myself.

Jez already knew he was heading to Rotterdam. The management had told him a few weeks earlier. He was 36 years old, in his 15th season as a professional, and was about to start his first Tour. He'd had the chance before, when riding for Banesto in the late 1990s, but he'd turned it down because he thought he was too young and feared it might burn him out, and because he was confident the opportunity would come round again soon enough. He'd had to wait another 13 summers.

Jez said: 'Don't you ever pass up the chance to ride the Tour de France.'

I accepted.

* * *

Four days later, I arrived in northern France to meet up with the rest of the Cervélo team. There were our two team leaders – the quiet, unassuming Spaniard, Carlos Sastre, Tour champion just two years earlier, and Thor Hushovd. Andreas Klier, an experienced German who knew the roads of Europe so well he was like a human sat-nav, was our captain-on-the-road. We were an international bunch with Xavier Florencio, of Spain, an Aussie, Brett Lancaster, Volodymir Gustov of Ukraine, Ignatas Konovalovas of Lithuania, and Jez Hunt and me from Britain.

Although the Tour started in Rotterdam, we were in the north-eastern corner of France ahead of the race to look at the cobbles we would face during stage three from Wanze to Arenberg. We knew it would be an important day for both our team leaders. Thor had targeted it as a possible stage win, and we'd need to protect Carlos on the cobbles because he would be vulnerable and we didn't want him to lose any time overall.

The final few days before the prologue time trial

felt like an eternity. Hanging around the hotel requires some skilful boredom management. I couldn't do too much riding because nothing I did now would help me during the Tour. Looking back at my racing programme over the previous few months, there was no way I was under-trained; in fact, there was every chance I'd run out of gas and the volume of racing would catch up with me, so I decided that I needed to start the Tour as fresh as possible.

I got a text from Adrian Timmis, who completed the Tour in 1987 for the British ANC-Halfords squad, and whose career was scarred by that experience. He advised me to do as little as possible in the days before the race. So I was taking resting to a whole new level, which gave me plenty of time to feel the build-up of nerves.

I was never a confident, bullish rider. I always doubted my ability, although I wasn't negative about it. I suppose I always feared the worst but hoped for the best. No one was expecting me to win a stage or anything like that, but I was always worried about letting down my team-mates. After all, a *domestique* who's unable to do his job is no use to anyone.

At the two editions of the Giro d'Italia I'd done, my job had been to stick by Carlos's side all the time. I'd ride in the wind, giving him a bit of shelter, enabling him to save a bit of energy that, over the course of a week on the flat roads, all adds up. When the road began to climb, I'd drop back and he would float away to participate in the actual race.

At this Tour, I had another role – to be an early link in Thor's lead-out train to help win a stage and score points towards defending the green jersey he'd won the previous year. So I had my hands full.

Everything began to feel real after I'd been handed my first set of race numbers – 99 – and the route book for the Tour, allowing me to pore over the maps of the stages, study the climbs. On the page, the gradients of the big cols, expressed in percentages, were just numbers that floated over me. There'd be plenty of time for what those numbers meant to hit me later in the race.

A couple of nights before the prologue, we had the traditional team presentation – a chance for the public to see all the Tour riders. Before the presentation, we gathered in a large auditorium to listen to a talk by Christian Prudhomme, who welcomed us to the Tour and talked us through what was expected of us during the race. My mind drifted back a decade to the pre-race talks I'd heard at amateur races in Britain. An instruction not to cross the white line in the middle of the road, a request not to chuck litter in the hedgerow, and a reminder that tea and coffee would be available in the community centre afterwards.

As if my stomach was not doing somersaults already, they then dimmed the lights and played a montage video of highlights from the previous year's race on the big screen. It gave me goosebumps, not least because one of the main protagonists in the 2009 Tour, Andy Schleck, was sitting just in front of me. The filmed showed them riding up Mont Ventoux, a stage I'd watched on television, and Brad Wiggins appeared on the screen. He'd ridden brilliantly that day to confirm fourth place overall – then the joint-best performance by a British rider. He was sitting a little to my right with his Sky team-mates and staff. As his image dominated the screen, I glanced across at him. He showed no emotion. There was barely a flicker of recognition on his face. It was as if he was looking through the screen rather than at it. If I had goosebumps, how was he feeling? He probably had the weight of the world on his shoulders.

It all felt unreal as we left the auditorium and emerged, blinking, into the light, as if we'd just left the cinema having watched a film that had read us our fortune. We went to get changed into our kit ready for the presentation. I was determined to soak up as much of the race as I could because in the back of my mind I thought it might be my only opportunity to experience it. The Tour had not been part of my race programme until the last minute. I was almost 30, so this could be it. My one and only Tour.

When it was Cervélo's turn to take to the stage, we got on our bikes and rolled over the bridge to the podium where we were to be presented to the crowds. The whole thing was being shown live on television so, as we rode over the bridge, a camera-man was following us.

I could feel my phone vibrating in my back pock-et with messages from friends and family who were watching. The cameras were focusing on Carlos and Thor, of course, and I always felt these presentations could be a bit embarrassing for the 'lesser' riders. Perhaps that's just my nature.

Michel Wuyts, who presents the cycling coverage on television in Belgium, had the job of introducing the riders one by one, giving a brief run-down of their achievements.

He started with Carlos. 'Winner of the 2008 Tour de France, three grand-tour stage wins, 13 times in the top ten at the grand tours…'

Then moved on to Thor. 'Double winner of the green jersey, winner of the Tour de France prologue and stages of all three grand tours, Norwegian na-tional road race champion…'

Eventually, Wuyts got to me. 'Silver-medallist at the British national championships…'

Actually, I can't remember exactly what he said. I think I managed to close my ears. Perhaps he said nothing at all, just introduced me as 'Daniel Lloyd'. Either way, I wanted to get off the stage quickly.

Afterwards, my wife, Lorraine, called.

'You looked really nervous, like a rabbit in the headlights.'

Yes, that pretty much sums it up.

The excitement was cut short.

Later that evening, the entire team, including the staff, was asked to attend a meeting in one of the conference rooms at the hotel. We didn't know what the meeting was about, but the tone of the email suggested it was something serious.

As I entered the room, I immediately clocked the glum faces. Our team manager, Joop Alberda, and Cervélo owner Gerard Vroomen were standing at the front, in silence, waiting for the last people to come in. Eventually the door was closed. I noticed one rider was missing. Xavier Florencio was not at the meeting.

We were told that Xavier had been treating a saddle sore with a cream that contained ephedrine. He hadn't realised that ephedrine had been recently placed on the banned list. [Note: ephedrine had been on WADA's monitoring programme since 2004, but was not banned until January 1, 2010.]

Cervélo's internal anti-doping policy was clear. We weren't allowed to use anything on the banned list, but we also were not allowed to use any medication without clearing it with the team doctor first.

Xavier hadn't tested positive, but he knew he'd used this cream and that ephedrine would be in his system for a few days, which meant there was the risk of it showing up if he was tested in the first week.

The deadline to call up a replacement rider had passed, so the management knew that if they took the right action we'd have to start the Tour with eight riders instead of nine.

Looking back, I feel it was a commendable thing for the team to do, and completely contrary to the way it might have been done in the years before. Cervélo's founders, Gerard Vroomen and Phil White, had set out to have a completely clean team, and there were to be no grey areas in a case like this. They could have quietly sent Xavier home and told the press he was unwell, but they didn't. Although it probably looked bad to the press and the public, it was the right thing to do. We felt bad for Xavier because I believe it was a genuine mistake, but the decision the management took was correct.

But it put a dampener on things. Doing the right thing risked making the team look like it was the subject of yet another doping scandal. All they could do was be as open and clear about the circumstances as they could, and hope people understood.

* * *

Prologue day was overcast. It rained on and off. Sky, famously, used their 'information hub caravanette' to predict that it would be dry for the early part of the prologue, so they gave Brad an early start time. I started about 15 minutes after Brad, and it had been pissing down for a good half-hour. Weather 1, Sky 0.

That morning, I had done a few laps of the

course. It wasn't particularly technical; the course was all about who had the most power. I think I'd have preferred technical. Our start times were stuck next to the door of the team bus and our bikes were lined up on home trainers under the awning, so we could start our warm-up routine when we were ready.

I started my warm-up and put my headphones on so I could concentrate and get into the zone, but there were so many distractions around me I had trouble blocking them out. There were crowds of people around the bus, gawping at us like we were in the zoo. Riders were passing in front of me, either heading out to the start ramp or coming back after their race. Dave Zabriskie was to my left, outside the Garmin bus, and he looked totally relaxed, as if he'd managed to reduce all the surroundings to nothing.

I wasn't helped by the fact my legs felt particularly average. The time passed slowly, just as it always does when I'm riding on the home trainer.

Finally it was time to get back on the bus to put my helmet and mitts on, and then get some help putting my arms through the top part of my skinsuit. The skinsuits are so tight these days that it's often a two-man job to actually get the thing on.

And then it was time to go.

At the start area, the commissaires checked my bike to make sure it met the regulations. I had a swig of water, gave my thermal jacket to our mechanic and rode up onto the start ramp.

I put my front wheel on the line, checked I was in the right gear then signalled to the starter that I was ready. He held my bike as I clipped my other foot in. I pressed the reset button on my computer (yes, I'm anal), took a few deep breaths and then looked out.

There was a TV cameraman to my left, a host of photographers to the right and a huge crowd lining the barriers all the way up the road ahead of me. Inside the start house there's a clock, so you can see the numbers count down until it is time to go.

The starter also tells you how long there is to go before doing the final countdown. It's in French, which makes it feel all the more exotic.

Trente.

Deep breath. Then another.

Dix.

This is it. The Tour de France.

Cinq, quatre, trois, deux, un, partez.

I had nothing. I am not a prologue specialist, so I wasn't expecting to fly round the circuit, but I could tell straight away I was going nowhere very fast. I felt weak, my breathing was laboured and my heart rate was high. The holy trinity of mediocrity.

When I crossed the line, despite being one of the early starters, I was already a long way down on the leaders. I was hugely disappointed. When the final results were in, I saw I was in the last 20 – and three of those behind me had crashed. I noted later that I'd only lost four seconds to Thor. Strange – and sad – as it sounds, I drew a certain consolation from the fact that my team-mate, a former Tour prologue winner, had also done badly. I didn't tell him that, of course, and if you see him don't let on either. It was not a great start but the dream was under way.

* * *

The first road stage was going to be nervous because the open roads from Holland towards Brussels were sure to be windy. Everyone in the bunch had something to lose, which meant there would be 197 riders all fighting to stay at the front, out of trouble. A dog ran into the peloton early on, which didn't do much to calm us down. Eventually we turned away from the coast and onto more sheltered roads so the anxiety was turned down from 11 for a bit.

When we crossed the border into Belgium, the crowds suddenly doubled or trebled in size. They were the biggest crowds I'd ever seen for a bike race and it was an awesome sight, and sound. We rode through a corridor of noise for kilometres.

It was then I realised how much we rely on all our senses in a bike race. Being able to hear is essential. At some point, there was a crash in the bunch. Normally, I'd have heard the sound of metal (and bone) on tarmac, I'd have heard the shouts and the curses, and I'd have had time to react. This time, I couldn't hear anything over the constant cheers, so the first I knew of the crash was when riders in front of me were braking hard and swerving.

A little later, a former team-mate of mine, Serge Pauwels, who was now riding for Team Sky, launched himself off the front of the bunch. It wasn't an attack, he just wanted to go ahead so he could spend a few seconds with his family, who had come out from their home town nearby to see him. It's a long-respected custom in the Tour. When he rejoined the bunch, I got chatting to him. This was his first Tour, too, so we compared our (limited) experiences.

Then I asked him about his new team and he hesitated. 'Yeah, it's okay…'

He sounded uncertain, so I prodded a little more.

'Well, I preferred it at Cervélo. For me, it's too much in this team. They are trying to do things too differently. I mean, if they could re-invent hot water, they would.'

Serge rides for Omega Pharma these days.

We knew the finish in Brussels would be a sprint. The break had been brought back, so the whole peloton was together. Garmin had spent most of the day working on the front of the bunch, and our tactic was to get to the front with about eight kilometres to go to keep Thor out of trouble and leave him with Brett Lancaster when HTC inevitably took over and started the final lead-out for Cavendish. My job started with six kilometres to go. I hit the front just after Fabian Wegmann of Milram peeled off. I had to keep the pace high and steady, and step it up a bit if anyone did try to take a flyer.

The goosebumps came again. It struck me that I was leading the Tour de France. Okay, it might not have meant much to some of the other riders in the race, but I will never those brief moments when I led the Tour.

There were a few crashes on the run-in. Cav was taken out and Thor ended up third behind the winner, Alessandro Petacchi. I crossed the line a much happier person than I'd been 24 hours earlier.

It was then I experienced the media scrum for the first time. When you're riding the race, you think about nothing beyond the finish line. The finish line is the goal, and so what happens afterwards seems to strike us afresh every day. Once we've got over the line and cruised to a halt, there's a huge crush of riders, our team helpers (*soigneurs*), cameramen, journalists, radio reporters. When you're tired, hot and thirsty, all you want to do is get back to the bus, but it can take ages to weave through the crowd. I've never had a microphone shoved in my face straight after a Tour stage, but I can see why Cav finds it hard some days. He's just poured everything out in the sprint, and within seconds people are asking questions and he's being jostled here and there.

That evening, two of my sisters came to see me at the hotel. I could see how proud they were of me, which made me feel really good. Just as they were about to leave, someone came over and asked me for an autograph. They laughed because they thought I'd set it up, but I hadn't!

* * *

The second road stage took us 201 kilometres through the hills of the Ardennes to Spa. Thor had identified this as another good one to score points towards the green jersey on because he felt some of the other sprinters might get dropped on the climbs.

We had our usual meeting on the bus before the start and decided we'd control the race once the break had gone clear. My job was to stick with Thor through the latter part of the stage, which was quite some responsibility. Riding on the front early in the stage is hard, but you can do it even if you're not feeling super. The risk of having a job late in the stage is that if I had a bad day I might be dropped before my duties even started.

Everything was going perfectly. A break of eight had gone away and we controlled the bunch, along with Stuart O'Grady from Saxo Bank, and gradually brought the gap down. As we reached the hills, I stuck to Thor like glue. I felt comfortable – almost in my element. I wasn't good in the mountains, but these five-minute climbs suited me. We neared the top of the Côte de Stockeu, one of the hills made famous by the Liège-Bastogne-Liège Classic, and, as we approached the summit, I rolled past Thor, to show him I was still there and feeling strong so he knew he could rely on me.

The rain had started by now and, as we began to go down the other side, I was in the first ten, just behind the Schlecks. Then disaster struck. Both Schlecks went down and, in my attempt to swerve round them, I also slipped on the oily surface and hit the floor. How Thor got past me without falling is beyond me, but he's not known as one of the best bike-handlers for nothing.

The race sped past me. Other riders fell on the greasy surface. I picked myself up and examined my injuries. Nothing broken but I'd grazed my right hip, elbow and knee, and strained my groin and wrist.

It was mayhem now. Riders were scattered everywhere. There were team cars trying to get past. Horns honking, people shouting. I knew my day was over. I thought there was no way I could get back to the front of the race now.

Little did I know that Fabian Cancellara, a team-mate of the Schlecks, had managed to neutralise the race so they could get back to the group. After some discussions, the commissaires decided to neutralise the race and cancel the time losses and points for the day – except for Sylvain Chavanel, who had been well ahead before the crash and was on his way to the stage win and yellow jersey. To this day I don't know why they didn't neutralise the time but still allow the riders to sprint for the points on offer. It was bad news for Thor because he could have scored well there.

Stage three, over the cobbles to Arenberg, was the one we'd been ready for. I never got to ride Paris-Roubaix – one of the downsides of being in such a strong Classics team – so I was very happy to experience the *pavé*.

My cuts and bruises weren't causing me any trouble, but my groin was painful. I couldn't pedal properly or sit comfortably on the bike. The start of the stage was incredibly fast, too, so I just had to grit my teeth and get on with it.

Our job started with about 50 kilometres to go, and I started riding at the front with Andreas and Ignatas to bring the break back and set up the finale. Quick Step were there with us because they were defending Chavanel's yellow jersey.

I slipped back a bit as we started to hit the cobbled sections. We'd got Thor into position and now it was up to him. I kept my earpiece in so I could listen to the conversation between my team-mates and the team car over the radio. There's not a running commentary, but you can piece together what's happening up ahead pretty well.

As we approached another section of cobbles I heard Andreas yell to Brett: 'Go, go, go. As hard as you can. Now!'

That was the moment that started the move

containing Thor, Cancellara, Geraint Thomas and a few others who eventually contested the finish.

My race was done when I was caught behind a crash on the really nasty stretch at Sars-et-Rosières, when it all bunched up a bit and we lost contact. On the side of the road there was a crowd of photographers, motorbikes parked up on the verge and a body lying in the gutter. I saw his Luxembourg national champion's jersey and knew his race was probably over, but there wasn't time to think of anything other than: 'Shit, that's Frank Schleck.'

I must have been out of range by the time Thor crossed the line, so I didn't hear the finish on the radio, but there's always someone who manages to pick up the info, and word eventually reached me that he'd won the stage. Sometimes, in the mountains, when you're struggling up the last climb, with half an hour or more still to climb, someone in the *gruppetto* will tell you who's won. I always think: 'Christ, they've finished already?'

But that day, I was delighted to hear the result, and it made the last 12 minutes of my ride pass that little bit more sweetly. That evening, there were smiles and Champagne at the dinner table, and a Norwegian TV crew. It was a warm evening, and we sat outside and enjoyed the moment. It was easy to forget that we'd ticked off only four days, and that there were 19 to go until we reached Paris. I tried not to dwell on that for too long.

* * *

There's no choice but to settle into the rhythm of the Tour. It dictates to you, rather than the other way around. Every day feels pretty much the same. I tried to sleep as well as possible, eat well, conserve as much energy as possible, and in the little bit of down time keep in touch with Lorraine and my son, Ralf, to remind myself that normal life was still going on.

The seventh stage from Tournus to Station des Rousses marked the first major climbs of the race. As a non-climber, the aim is to do as much work for the team as possible early on, then slip back into the *gruppetto* – the large bunch of riders that gathers at the back of the race and rides in as comfortably and easily as possible. I say 'easily', but that's a relative term. It's not often comfortable or easy in the last group on the road because the clock is always ticking towards the time cut. But there's a sense of camaraderie back there because we're all in it together.

Things really lit up on the penultimate climb, the second-category Col de la Croix de la Serra, and not long after the start of it around 50 riders eased up slightly and relaxed. When we got to the top we were given an update on the time gap. The leaders were 16 minutes ahead of us.

Brett Lancaster came back to me with a concerned look on his face. 'D'ya know what the time limit will be today, Lloydy?'

'No – must be quite generous though.'

'I'm not so sure, mate. This is only a "medium-mountain" stage. I think we'd better check.'

For riders in the *gruppetto*, calculating the time cut is a preoccupation during the mountain stages. And it's not easy to work out. Each stage, the riders are given a time limit, and they have to make it to the finish inside that otherwise they risk elimination. (Usually the *gruppetto* is big enough that the organisers would not chuck out 40 or 50 riders, but riders can be deducted points for the green jersey, which would be disastrous for the sprinters, so no one wants to be outside.)

The limit depends on the severity of the stage, and is calculated as a percentage of the winner's time, using a formula based on the average speed of the winner. So, if the stage is won in a fast speed, the time cut is more generous.

Brett dropped back to the car to have a word with our second *directeur sportif*, Alex Sans Vega. I wasn't sure how accurate their sums were, but Brett was in a panic when he came back to us.

By the time we'd realised how close it was going to be, we were running out of kilometres, so Brett, Jez and I got to the front and started pushing it hard on the descent, then set a good tempo on the last climb, the Côte de Lamoura. Then we heard Robbie McEwen shouting.

'What the fuck are ya doing Bert? [Robbie always

called Brett Bert.] We've got loads of time – slow the fuck down.'

We ignored him and pressed on. Robbie was pissed off that the pace was so hard because his team-mate Stijn Vandenberghe had been dropped and was all on his own. We knew our group was big enough to avoid elimination, but we didn't want to cost Thor any green jersey points, especially as Petacchi was a few minutes further up the road.

That night, we got the results sheets delivered to the hotel, as every team does, and found we'd finished 22 minutes and 17 seconds behind Sylvain Chavanel – less than a minute inside the time cut. Vandenberghe had been eliminated and Brett got a text from Robbie, apologising.

Next morning, we had a Dutch TV crew on the bus, filming a short documentary. We had our team meeting about an hour before the start, and Jean-Paul, who's Dutch, gave it.

'Okay guys, before we get to today's stage, I just want to do a short recap of yesterday. You all did a good job. Carlos was put in the position he needed to be. Well done. The rest of you did your jobs and then made it inside the time limit comfortably…'

A voice piped up – I'm not sure who it was – with: 'We made it by less than a minute, Jean-Paul! It didn't feel very comfortable!'

I could see Jean-Paul was irate at being shown up in front of the TV crew, knowing that this moment

would go out in his home country. He was silent for
a few seconds, but kept smiling so he didn't show his
annoyance. Even if the cameras had been shooting
in black and white they'd have noticed his skin had
gone bright red with embarrassment.

The eighth stage to Morzine was a real struggle
for me, and the rest day couldn't come soon enough.
My legs actually felt good, but my groin was getting
more painful. I was taking painkillers (legal ones) to
try to reduce the discomfort. It took ages for the
break to go clear that day, and I was starting to think
my Tour might be over soon. Every time we went
round a corner, and on every short climb, I was in
danger of getting dropped. I couldn't get the power
out of my legs because of the soreness in my groin.

Days like that are horrible. I was at the back of
the peloton, where it's a constant fight to stay in contact with the rider in front. I was just hoping that the
front of the bunch would let a group go so we could
ease off a little bit. Cyclists use the phrase 'a world of
pain' a lot, but that day was agonising for me.

* * *

A rest day in the Alps. Could there be a more beautiful place to take a break? By this point I was sharing
a room with Andreas, who was so experienced and
tactically astute that the management often came
up to the room to ask his thoughts. He had been

sharing with Thor, but I think Thor got fed up with the constant interruptions from the sports directors and wanted a couple of days to himself.

Every rider's rest day routine is different. Some riders prefer not to disrupt the rhythm and will go out for four hours. I would just do an easy hour or hour-and-a-half with the team just to keep loose. I never felt the need to do more.

Andreas and I had a nice room (always a bonus on the Tour) with a balcony overlooking the mountains. In the evening, we ordered a bottle of wine and sat on the balcony listening to music, watching the heavy clouds cross the mountains. We could see flashes of lightning in the distance as the rain moved in.

Andreas told me a few of his stories (he's got a large catalogue) and we watched the world go by.

Below us, a strange house caught our attention. It seemed to be some sort of hippy commune and, over the course of an hour, all sorts of weird people were coming and going. That kept us amused for a while, imagining who they were and what was going on inside. It's amazing what your brain can conjure up when you're a week into a stage race.

* * *

The stages between the Alps and Pyrenees are some-times taken for granted by the fans, who think that because the battle for the yellow jersey dies down for a bit the race must be easy. For the *domestiques*, these can be some of the hardest days because there's not the security of the *gruppetto* to slip back to.

My job on days like these was to stay with Carlos, but that was often easier said than done. In the two editions of the Giro d'Italia I'd ridden, I'd realised that he's not a typical GC [general classification] rider. He doesn't want to be at the front unless it's absolutely necessary. During the 2009 Giro, it had surprised me how far back he'd start the important climbs. One day he'd started the final climb so far from the front that he was behind riders already calling '*gruppetto*'. When I finally crawled onto the team bus, I found he'd finished seventh, in a group with all the favourites.

On stage 12 to Mende, as we approached the first third-category climb, I was in the last ten with Carlos. There hadn't been a break, so we'd hit the climb 'full gas'. And I could tell I wasn't on a good day. About a kilometre into the climb, the bunch was in one long line. Carlos, sensing danger, calmly pulled out of the line and rode past everybody towards the front. His right-hand man – me – was stuck, unable to summon the strength to follow him.

Then the inevitable happened. A rider a few places ahead of me let the wheel go and I watched in despair as the gap opened, unhitching about ten of us from the freight train ahead. There were still 190 kilometres to go and we were in trouble.

By the time we got to the top of the climb, the team cars were coming past us and panic was setting in. We tried to get as much shelter as possible behind the cars. Effectively we were cheating because we'd been dropped fair and square – we weren't returning to the bunch after a puncture or a crash.

Soon enough we were 'out the arse' – as we eloquently put it when the peloton has left us behind – and I thought my luck was about to run out. I was cursing myself for starting the climb so far back.

It's surprisingly quiet and lonely back there. The crowds, thinking the whole show has passed them by, seem surprised to see you. We had one motorcycle outrider in front and the *voiture balai* – the dreaded broomwagon – behind.

We pressed on and, after what felt like an eternity, we saw the back of the convoy of cars and the dancing coloured dots of the peloton ahead of us. It's amazing how much it lifts the spirits when you finally have something in sight to chase. It gave us the impetus we needed to get back in contact. At kilometre 65, and after a 40-kilometre chase, we were back.

I felt a huge sense of relief, but immediately I felt sympathy with the club riders who get dropped on the climbs. Maybe you know the feeling of struggling to the top of a climb, where everyone has waited to regroup. As you reach them, they set off straight away before you've had a chance to catch your breath.

That's what happened to us that day. As soon as

we got back to the bunch, some team or other got to the front and started chasing the break.

* * *

The final week was about survival for me. The first week is so fast and aggressive, it seems impossible to imagine. But the last few days are even more intense. The battle to establish a break in the final week can rage for hours, for a number of reasons. The general classification is well established, which means that a break has a good chance of staying away to the finish, so everyone wants to be in it. And as Paris gets closer, there are usually a number of teams who have had very little success, so they are getting desperate.

On stage 15 from Pamiers to Bagnères-de-Luchon, it took 120 kilometres of non-stop attacking before a break was allowed to go clear. It was 48 kilometres per hour on lumpy roads for two-and-a-half hours.

Just getting into a position to be able to launch, or follow, an attack is hard enough. Some riders can respond to attack after attack – Juan Antonio Flecha springs to mind – but I know I have only one effort in me.

I had a free rein that day, and decided to have a go. I thought I'd made it when, after 110 kilometres, I got into a group of 15, but someone chased it down. The very next attack had Thomas Voeckler in it, and he went on to win the stage. It's a strange feeling when it takes so long for a break to form, especially if you've been trying to get in it. After two-and-a-half hours of high-speed racing, the move that goes suddenly feels like a soft one, and we all slow down to 20 kilometres per hour.

Before I turned pro, I assumed the riders who made the break were the ones who had decided that morning to go for it. Little did I realise that, often, three-quarters of the bunch has tried, and failed, to be part of it.

* * *

Going into the second rest day, in Pau, Thor had the green jersey – but only just. He'd performed heroics the previous day, hauling his 84-kilogram frame over the mountains to win the bunch sprint in Pau and collect six crucial points.

But we knew Thor was not faster than Petacchi on the flat finishes and, with Bordeaux and Paris to come, the Italian had the edge. Thor knew it and we knew it, but our team manager Joop Alberda had other ideas. Joop had not been a pro cyclist but he'd coached other sports, including volleyball and tennis, and worked with the Dutch Olympic team. On the rest day, he called Andreas and me to his room.

'I want to show you something,' he said, opening his laptop and calling up YouTube.

He played us a clip of Michael Chang playing Ivan Lendl in the 1989 French Open. We watched as Chang, completely out of the blue, served under-arm, catching Lendl off guard and winning the point.

'Sometimes, gentlemen, you need to think differently, outside the box, in order to win,' Joop said. 'Go away and think about how we are going to win that green jersey.'

Andreas, one of the smartest tactical brains around, had used every trick in the book. As far as we were concerned, Thor staying with the climbers over the Aubisque to win unlikely points in Pau had been the equivalent of Chang's under-arm serve. There were no more rabbits to pull from the hat.

* * *

Having climbed the Tourmalet before the rest day, we had to do it from the other direction the day after the rest day. Carlos had not been riding as well as he had hoped. He was around 20th overall and had one last chance to win a stage. The plan was for one of us to get in the early breakaway, then, once it was established, Carlos would jump across on one of the climbs knowing that he had a team-mate up ahead who could then drill it for as long as possible to give him a chance of then taking the stage.

The problem was, no one had been strong enough, or savvy enough, to get into the break.

There's a knack to getting in those breaks, and I'm still not certain I'm the best person to explain what that knack is.

Basically, the break went, and then a couple of teams who had men in the break then used the narrow roads to block anyone else from the bunch springing across. They do that by simply riding at the front and filling the width of the road so no one can come past. They knock the pace off a bit and, before you know it, the break is a minute up the road, making it very hard for individual riders to get across.

Once the break had gone, Carlos was absolutely mad. He was shouting over the radio that we had to attack and get someone in the break. Usually so calm and quiet, I'd never heard him raise his voice before. I could tell he was deadly serious, but I was pinned where I was, three rows back, unable to go forward.

Carlos kept shouting. Poor Jean-Paul didn't know what to say. I managed to squeeze into the second row, just behind Bernie Eisel. I asked him if he'd let me through so I could go up the road to take a piss. He opened the door and I attacked as hard as I could. I heard the angry shouts and abuse from the riders at the front of the bunch. I knew I'd be ridiculed, but I respected Carlos and didn't want to let him down.

Somehow Caisse d'Epargne's Jose Ivan Gutierrez managed to follow me, and we set off after the break, which was two minutes ahead by now.

We closed in on the break, but the bunch was

closing in on us, too, which meant it was working out okay for Carlos. The bunch caught Gutierrez and me, and, just as they did, Carlos attacked with Vladi.

What followed was excruciating. Vladi buried himself to try to close the gap, but soon faded leaving Carlos to chase alone on the next climb. He was alone, stuck in no man's land. He got to within striking distance of them by the top of the climb, but never made contact. Then he rode on, alone, over the Marie-Blanque and Soulor. For a rider of his stature – a man who'd won the Tour only two years previously – it was incredibly humiliating, and I felt bad for him, but there wasn't anything more I could have done.

Carlos was particularly quiet after the stage, even for him, but the next morning he spoke up.

We still had a job to do for Thor, and the team talk was all about how we could help him score points and win the day's flat stage to Bordeaux.

Then Carlos stood up. 'I would like to say a few words. Before I start, Andreas, would you please take off your shades – I want to see your eyes.'

The tension in the team had been rising. Andreas was the team's key tactician, and his focus had been on helping Thor win the green jersey, which was an achievable aim. It's not unfair to say Andreas had not been as busy helping Carlos in the mountains.

By asking Andreas to take off his sunglasses, Carlos was making it clear he was talking to him.

'I want to talk to you boys about the past three weeks,' Carlos said calmly. 'I am not happy. Without me, this team would not have been invited to this race. I have won here before, but have been shown little respect. I only had two riders here for me, and one of them was sent home before the race started.

'Vladi, you haven't been good enough. I needed more from you in the mountains, and I know you can do better.

'For the rest of you, I feel you've concentrated on the flatter days. For the mountains you've talked more about how you're going to get inside the time limit than how you're going to help me. This is not how a professional team of our level should be thinking. I expected more from all of you.'

Jean-Paul tried to interrupt Carlos midway through without success.

I felt bad for Carlos. I respected him, and to this day hold him in very high regard. He is the most modest of champions, unassuming and easy-going, but he was clearly very frustrated.

The person I felt most sorry for was Vladi. I'd not come across a more dedicated *domestique*, and he'd been with Carlos since their days with the CSC team. I think he was taken aback.

The problem was not what Carlos had said, but the timing of his speech. We were less than an hour away from the start of a very important stage – one which could help set Thor up for the green jersey.

I'm not sure about the others, but it killed my con-
centration, and I was genuinely upset that Carlos
thought I had not done enough for him.

* * *

It's hard to describe the feelings I had as we took the
train from Bordeaux to Paris on the final Sunday of
the Tour. I knew Lorraine and Ralf would be waiting,
and that I'd be emotional seeing them.

If it hadn't been the Tour, I don't think I'd have
made it. I was having terrible pain with staphylococ-
cus – a painful bacterial infection that wasn't going
to get better while I was racing my bike. I had seven
spots on my legs, and they were getting bigger by
the day. It was getting so painful that just putting
my tracksuit bottoms on was agony if the material
brushed against my skin.

The final stage into Paris was like the last day of
term but, in reality, the season wasn't over. I'd be racing again in a few weeks, back on the same bus, but
it felt like the end of something significant. I'd also
grown closer to the riders and staff than I had at
previous races. The final stage, arriving on the
Champs-Élysées and crossing the line, passed in a
blur. I tried to commit all the details to memory, but
it was just a bit overwhelming.

The day after the Tour, I felt lost. Lorraine, Ralf
and I had a late flight home, so we had a day to spend